CHOSEN

ROBERT J. WATKINS

BRIDGE
LOGOS

Newberry, FL 32669

Bridge-Logos
Newberry, FL 32669

Chosen: Become the Person You Were Meant to Be
by Dr. Robert J. Watkins

Printed in the United States of America

Library of Congress Catalog Card Number: 2019932110

International Standard Book Number: 978-1-61036-407-2

Cover/Interior design by Kent Jensen | knail.com

Editorial Director: Dr. Larry Keefauver

VP 01 07/2019

DEDICATION

This book is dedicated to my smart, brilliant, beautiful, and ingenious daughters,

Gabrielle and Noelle.

Thank you for challenging me to be a better person. I love you both so much.

ACKNOWLEDGMENTS

I gratefully acknowledge and express deep appreciation to the many wonderful people who made this project possible:

Sherile Thorne, for listening and writing down my stories on paper. She helped me get over my fear of disclosing my deepest secrets so I can begin to help you, the reader. Thank you, Sherile.

Sandra Fuller, for her faithful dedication to our vision, and for serving the people who depend on our counsel, guidance, and wisdom every day.

The Conquer members, partners, and associates, who have supported us for over twenty years.

Most of all, God, for choosing me to make a difference in the world, and for not giving up on me when I did not deserve mercy.

FOREWORD

Chosen has special meaning and focus in the words of Christ. He taught, *"For many are called, but few are chosen"* (Matthew 22:14 KJV). Are you chosen? That's tantamount to asking ourselves:

"Am I special?"

"What am I supposed to be doing with my life?"

"Does anyone care particularly for me?"

"Does God, who created me, have a particular purpose, calling, or legacy for just me?"

"What does it mean to be chosen?"

Dr. Watkins' treatment of God's purposes behind choosing you in particular for certain tasks, vocations, and relationships is thoughtful, challenging, inspiring, and revelatory for you. You will discover in the pages of this book that you can become the person you were meant to be.

In *Christianese*, we often talk about those who are "lost" versus those who are "saved." May I suggest that many who are *saved* often struggle with being *lost*? As a pastoral counselor, I have listened to hundreds of clients—born-again believers—who feel lost, hopeless, and helpless. They don't know who they are *in Christ*.

Lost believers are those who have lost a sense of calling, purpose, and direction in their work, relationships, and personal spiritual journeys. Sadly, those feeling lost have never heard the very real words of Jesus spoken to their spirit, "I have chosen you."

Being *chosen* goes beyond:

- Being a good person or a good Christian.
- Being smart or wise.
- Being called into a certain vocation or position of leadership.

As you read this book, Dr. Watkins will unpack for you a personal understanding of how God has chosen you in such a way that your life will be changed and impacted. Being chosen will so brand you that not only will success and prosperity grace your life, you will also step into *significance*—making a difference in everything you say and do.

If you hunger for this deep revelation, which will impact both your present journey and your eternal destiny, then read on.

—Dr. Larry Keefauver, Bestselling Author
and International Teacher

TABLE OF CONTENTS

INTRODUCTION

Everybody wants to be chosen for something.

You did not choose Me, but I chose you, and appointed you that you should go and bear fruit. (John 15:16a NASB)

As a small and scrawny eight-year-old, I wanted to play football and basketball with the older kids in my neighborhood. I lived right across the street from the park, so I would show up in my brand new white Converse tennis shoes, my red shorts, and white t-shirt hoping the big kids would choose me.

I would try to show off in hope that they would select me to be on the team, but nobody did. I remember how I felt, and it wasn't a good feeling. When I went to school, I auditioned to be an actor in a production, but I wasn't chosen for that either.

Most people want to be chosen for something special. There are people in ministry who want to be chosen to preach the gospel. There are people in business who want their product or service to be chosen over their competitor's. When it comes to relationships, people want to be chosen by someone who loves them.

For many are called, but few are chosen. (Matthew 22:14 KJV)

Since many are called but few are chosen, who are the *chosen ones?* They are the individuals who show up to do the work they are called to do. You have a role to play in order to be chosen. God chose you to do something great, but you have to show up.

The little kid with the red shorts, white t-shirt, and Converse tennis shoes kept showing up at the basketball court. And after his skills got better—and after he got a little taller—eventually, he was chosen. But he had to show up and play hard.

> WHO ARE THE CHOSEN?
> THEY ARE THE INDIVIDUALS WHO SHOW UP TO
> DO THE WORK THEY ARE CALLED TO DO.

Some people feel they are *less than enough* when it comes to feeling they can perform a task. They feel insecure or fearful. And when it comes to being chosen for Christ's team, those are the reasons they don't believe they've been chosen to be a light in this world. If that is you, this book will help you move beyond your insecurities and fear.

But beyond your ability to answer God's call, you may be in midlife and feel that, since you have been divorced, you don't know how to choose the right mate. Not only will you learn in this book how to be chosen, you will also learn how to choose.

I want to show you how to get everything you need in your life and accept what God has for you. This may sound simple, but many people still don't know how to receive all God has for them.

> IT WASN'T UNTIL I SAW MYSELF AS
> GOD SAW ME THAT I KNEW I WAS CHOSEN
> TO DO A GREAT WORK.

I am sure that even as an orphaned baby, I sensed a need to be chosen by parents who would love me. Then one day, the executive director of an orphanage in downtown Detroit made the decision to do a television promotion in the hope that the little boys would be adopted. There were too many kids in the orphanage to be taken care of properly, and the goal was for them to be seen by potential parents.

In the little town of Monroe, Michigan, there was a couple who wanted to conceive a child, but the wife was barren. She was at home vacuuming, saw the advertisement on television, and a particularly cute little boy caught her eye. She turned off the vacuum cleaner and wrote down the number. It wasn't until three weeks later when she convinced her husband to drive about an hour and a half to the orphanage.

They met with the executive director and asked to see the little boys. One by one she looked at them but told the director she didn't see the one she was looking for. As they sadly turned to leave, the executive director brought out one more baby boy they had overlooked. She laid her eyes on me and said, "This is the cute little boy I was looking for."

Six months later, the adoption process was completed, and they brought me home.

Later, I found out my birth mother was a teenager, and I could have easily been aborted. The fact that God allowed me to stay alive is why I believe I was chosen for something supernatural.

I equate my life's story to another famously adopted little boy. His name was Moses. Moses was adopted by royalty and became the *Prince of Egypt*. Even though he was born in slavery, he was chosen to be a deliverer. I believe that I, too, am chosen to be a deliverer. Through my ministry and business, I help deliver others from financial bondage.

DO YOU KNOW WHAT YOU HAVE BEEN CHOSEN
TO DO? DO YOU KNOW THAT UNDERSTANDING
WHAT YOU WERE CHOSEN TO DO CAN HAVE A
POWERFUL BENEFIT IN YOUR LIFE?

Studies have shown that people with a sense of purpose had a fifteen percent lower risk of an early death compared with those who admitted they were more or less aimless in life. And it didn't matter when people found their direction or purpose—whether it was in their twenties, fifties, or seventies.[1]

This is great news, because that means it's never too late for you to start moving in the direction of your calling. Even if you feel like you missed your ship when it docked, you can still swim out to get to it. You are reading this book for a reason. You were chosen, and it's time to discover what it is you are supposed to be doing from this point forward.

YOU HAVE AN ASSIGNMENT. YOU ARE TO
COMPLETE IT AND RECEIVE A REWARD FROM IT.

Deep down within your core, you know you have been chosen, but you don't know how to navigate to what comes next. This discovery process is exciting. You are going to finally *discover* what it is you are supposed to be doing, *decide* how to do it, and *develop* into it. Here are six clues to get you started toward discovering your God-designed call, purpose, and assignment.

---

1   https://www.npr.org/sections/health-shots/2014/07/28/334447274/
    people-who-feel-they-have-a-purposein-life-live-longer

1. **Where are you willing to invest all your time and money?** Wherever you are willing to invest your time and treasure is a clue. Is it with the homeless, the elderly, or the needy? Do you like visiting hospitals or nursing homes to give an encouraging word? Do you like cleaning and cooking?

2. **If you could teach three things to the next generation, what would those things be?** Maybe you should teach, write books, or both.

3. **What don't you like?** Compassion and sensitivity to certain things are also signs. Whatever makes you cry or angers you is a clue to what you are assigned to address and rectify. Do poverty, women's issues, or perhaps mistreatment of animals make you angry?

4. **Who is always in your space?** Who's drawn to you? Do you always find yourself around a certain person, or a certain group of people, who needs your help? Your assignment may be to a person or a group of people. You must identify who he/she is, or who they are, and how you are to minister to or help them.

5. **What would you do for free?** If everybody on earth were told they could perform any task they wanted, and the payment would be food and shelter, what would you choose to do?

6. **What brings you peace of mind?** Peace is confirmation of the Holy Spirit being in agreement with your actions and decisions.

These questions will help you in your discovery process and show you in what direction you should steer your ship. Your focus, time, and energy need to be dedicated to what you discover you have been chosen to do. Remember, having a purpose adds years to your life, so it is very important that you follow through on this discovery process.

I believe you are reading this book because you know that you, too, are chosen for something great. Be relentless and unwavering in your faith. As you advance through these pages, your walk will turn into a jog, and then into a full-out sprint as your excitement about your calling increases.

My goal is that my transparency will encourage you on your quest to become the person you were meant to be.

> YOU HAVE BEEN CHOSEN
> FOR SUCH A TIME AS THIS.

You have been chosen as God's first and only choice to be the person only you can be, to accomplish the God-given assignments only you can do, and to impact the lives that the world needs to change eternally through *only you.*

Turn the page and let's begin your new journey.

CHAPTER 1

GET REAL WITH YOURSELF

Then you will know the truth, and the truth will set you free. (John 8:32 NIV)

Faking it until you make it is not a good strategy for becoming the person you were meant to be. Jesus said knowing the truth is what will set you free.[2] To know truth is to become so intimate with truth that it scorches and obliterates every lie, myth, or half-truth in your soul.

Are you ready for that?

In my youth, I knew I was adopted. My cousins and the neighborhood kids teased me because I was different. I didn't know who my real parents were. My defense was to make up a story about my birth parents. I dreamed my mother was a

---

2   "Then Jesus said to those Jews who believed Him, 'If you abide in My word, you are My disciples indeed. And you shall know the truth, and the truth shall make you free'" (John 8:31-32 NKJV).

beautiful actress and my father played professional football. After all, I believed I was a good actor, and I had a passion to be a football player.

I lied to myself about my real identity all through my teenage years and into adulthood. I struggled privately about why my own mother didn't want me and why my birth father walked away from me. Years later, the lies I told myself about my fake identity negatively affected all my relationships. Even my relationships with my daughters were not exempt. It wasn't until I got *real* with myself that my life began to change.

> WHETHER TO YOU IT'S UGLY OR PRETTY,
> TRUTH IS TRUTH.

FIX YOUR THOUGHT LIFE

I had no idea who I was, which brought confusion and lack of purpose in my life. The thoughts concerning my identity were a combination of fantasy, other people's opinions of me, and visions of what I wanted to be. Once I realized as a teenager that I didn't know who my real parents were, and that they gave me up for adoption, my immediate emotions were fear, anger, and loneliness.

In my mind, my mother was this beautiful actress named Diahann Carroll. Having an actress for a mother made sense to me because I believed I had a gift for performing. I figured that's where my genes came from. And I always wanted to be a professional football player, so I envisioned that my real father would be in the NFL.

My fantasy world was also a mental escape, because my surroundings continually reminded me that I was adopted by a working-class family. I couldn't wait to get out of that situation. It was self-deception. As I lied to myself, the obvious happened. I started lying to other people. I became a proficient liar as a teenager.

Have you ever met someone who exaggerates so much that they start believing their own lies? Well, I was exactly like that. When a person is in this kind of mental state and starts dating and getting into relationships, they'll start lying about things even when there's no reason to lie. They won't know what's real even when it's right in front of them. Then one generation starts passing a lying spirit on to the next generation.

I had to get free by accepting the truth. But in order to do that, I first had to fix my thoughts about myself. I stopped telling people that Diahann Carroll was my mother. I confessed that I didn't know who my birth mother was—and that I had never met her or my birth father. It took me a long time to admit it, because there was shame attached to the reality of my situation.

As a twenty-year-old, I realized I needed to fix my thought life, so I sought God and counseling. There are a lot of people who need to address their mental health issues but haven't done so because of the stigma concerning it.

There is nothing wrong with seeking godly counsel. In fact, it's one of the directions in your *life-manual*—the Word of God— that has been revealed to you many times. That means God is serious about making sure you understand the importance of seeking godly counsel.

> *The way of a fool is right in his own eyes, but a wise man is he who listens to counsel.* (Proverbs 12:15 NASB)

> *Where there is no counsel, the people fall; but in the multitude of counselors there is safety.* (Proverbs 11:14 NKJV)

There is safety in having the proper counseling. The Word of God says it can keep you from falling. Your thoughts lead to your actions, and your actions lead you to good or bad decisions—success or suffering. It is imperative that your thought life is in harmony with the Word of God.

You were chosen to do a good work, and the blueprint is already complete. You have a manual and handbook that is accessible to you twenty-four hours a day. Once you take on the mind of Christ, there is nothing that will be impossible for you.

I can do all things through Christ who strengthens me.
(Philippians 4:13 NKJV)

You have the strength to win the battle between the ungodly fantasies and the sacred thoughts that fight for your mind's attention. The war for your thoughts is a reality. Winning in this area is crucial to living a victorious life. You must take your thoughts captive and make them obedient to God.

We demolish arguments and every pretension that sets itself up
against the knowledge of God, and we take captive every thought
to make it obedient to Christ.
(2 Corinthians 10:5 NIV)

However, the roots of our thoughts come from the desires of our hearts. So to fix our *thought-lives* and renew our minds, we must address our *heart-lives*. The conditions of our hearts—our feelings and instincts—directly impact the nature of our thoughts. If we are dominated by a sinful nature, our thoughts will destroy us. But if we are controlled by the Holy Spirit, our thoughts will bring peace, joy, and life to us as well as to those who are connected to us.

Our thoughts are powerful, and the things we meditate on can affect our lives in a significant and sometimes detrimental way. They have the ability to bring forth feelings of anxiety, pain, and stress. With that being said, they also are quite capable of helping us feel good, comfortable, and peaceful.

We can choose to experience whatever we want through the thoughts we allow to play a part in the *movie* playing in our minds. We can foster healthy thoughts, but we can also play out unhealthy thoughts to our detriment. As I did with my make-believe mother, Diahann Carroll, we can create characters or scenarios that don't really exist!

Then we begin to believe the blockbuster movie playing in our mind—one that we created, produced, directed, and starred in. The budget was expensive, untamed thoughts.

The apostle Paul tells us in God's Word:

Do not be conformed to this world, but be transformed by the renewing of your mind, that you may prove what is that good and acceptable and perfect will of God. (Romans 12:2 NKJV)

Paul also said:

*And now, dear brothers and sisters, one final thing. **Fix your thoughts** on what is true, and honorable, and right, and pure, and lovely, and admirable. Think about things that are excellent and worthy of praise.*
(Philippians 4:8 NLT [emphasis mine])

These are the best instructions I can offer on how to fix your thought life: Whenever undesirable thoughts try to enter your mind, use the power God has given you to cast them out. Send them on their way, and give that space to God-approved mental matter.

CHANGE YOUR WORDS

How do you know if you need to fix your thought life? The answer is actually very simple. Just listen to the words that you speak. What you are thinking about eventually comes out in the spoken word.

"I'm on a fixed income."
"If it weren't for bad luck, I wouldn't have any."
"Every time I turn around something is going wrong."
"My wife gets on my nerves."
"My husband is annoying."
"My kids are Satan's seeds."

When you fix your thoughts, those words will change to:

"Wealth and riches are in my house. I expect daily increase."
"I'm blessed coming in and going out."
"All things are working for my good."
"My wife is a virtuous woman."
"My husband is a king and a priest."
"My children are world changers."

Notice, I didn't tell you to wait until you see your husband acting like a king to call him one. Call him a king in the midst of him acting like a clown, which will definitely get his attention. Neither did I tell you to wait until you get the six or seven figure check to call yourself wealthy.

Feeling *wealthy* is a mindset.

When you think *right* about a *wrong* situation, your words will be the foundation for the manifestation of what you desire to see changed. You can speak words of death, or you can speak words of life. We read in Proverbs, *"Death and life are in the power of the tongue."* [3] Remember, this world was **spoken** into existence!

3 Proverbs 8:21 (KJV).

YOUR THOUGHTS PRECEDED
EVERYTHING YOU HAVE DONE IN LIFE:
MIND TO MOUTH TO MANIFESTATION.

Thoughts from your mind exit your head through your mouth and then manifest themselves in your life. What you are manifesting could be good or bad; it depends on your thoughts. So many people speak negative things into their lives based on the thoughts they allow to travel between their ears. Speak positive affirmations over your life, family, business, and ministry. You don't need a prophet to tell you what to expect, you can prophesy to yourself.

We have the power and authority to control our thought lives by escorting the wrong thoughts out of our minds and depositing in our minds the right thoughts that come from the Word of God.

LISTEN TO YOUR OWN VOICE

After I graduated from high school, I remember coming home and my mom asking me what I wanted to do with my life. At the time, I had track-and-field scholarships, but I didn't want to go to college. I told her all I wanted to do is ride around and get high with my friends.

I got up the morning after my graduation celebration, and there was an Army recruiter sitting in the living room. My mother signed away my buttocks to the armed forces! I didn't have a choice in the matter. I was so scared! It was July, and I was leaving in September. I'd never been on an airplane before, and I had to fly to Fort Jackson, in South Carolina.

September came around quickly. And suddenly, I was in basic training. Sergeants were yelling at me—as they are conditioned to do.

We were in formation, and the drill sergeant said, "Private Watkins, front and center."

I approached him at the front of the squad, and he said, "Call the men to attention."

I turned around and said, "Platoon, attention!"

Those men snapped to attention. That's the first time I really heard my voice and saw a response to it. There was a corresponding action to a command I had given. I'll never forget how I felt when those men responded. It was a defining moment in my life. It was at that point when I knew there was something I was supposed to do—something greater than riding around with my friends and getting high.

That experience was so profound because I didn't think my voice mattered. I had always felt like nobody cared to hear what I had to say. I thought my voice was meaningless. I had always been insecure about my voice, because I didn't like how I sounded. I didn't think my voice was strong enough or had enough baritone in it.

When I started my ministry years later, the devil was still in my ear about my voice—trying to keep me feeling *less than enough*. Well, we serve an awesome God, who thought enough about me to use the very thing that I was insecure about to prosper me! My voice is now being heard all over the world.

I encourage you to listen to your own voice. Some may call it their inner voice. To others it is their intuition or a gut feeling. For me, it's the voice of the Holy Spirit. If your inner voice is telling you there is more to your life than what you are doing now, listen to it. If you are feeling like something is missing, listen to that *still small voice.*[4]

Go on your own *seek and find* mission to discover what your inner voice is directing you to do. Your gut feeling will lead you in the direction you are supposed to be going. Let that instinct be your compass. Even animals and children have intuition or instinct. Your voice is important, so listen to it. Your voice is powerful, and it matters.

> START BLOCKING OUT OTHER VOICES
> THAT SOUND OPPOSITE OF THE GOALS YOU WANT
> TO ACCOMPLISH ON YOUR WAY TO BECOMING WHO
> YOU WERE MEANT TO BE.

MOVE FROM PERCEPTION TO REALITY

What do you see when you look in the mirror? Most people have the wrong perception of themselves.

If you live in a 15,000 square foot mansion, have celebrity friends, drive fancy cars, and take expensive vacations, your perception of yourself, and the perception of others around you, may be that you have arrived. That may be your perception even though the reality of it is that you've got overwhelming debt, you've signed papers for a house that you really can't afford, and you're fearful that you're going to lose the possessions you have.

---

4   "Then He said, 'Go out, and stand on the mountain before the LORD.' And behold, the LORD passed by, and a great and strong wind tore into the mountains and broke the rocks in pieces before the LORD, but the LORD was not in the wind; and after the wind an earthquake, but the LORD was not in the earthquake; and after the earthquake a fire, but the LORD was not in the fire; and after the fire a still small voice" (1 Kings 19:11-12 NKJV).

You may think you're rich because you have a good-paying job or career through which you earn a million dollars a year. However, if you live like you make ten million dollars a year, you're not rich, you're broke. This concept is not just for the millionaire, it's the same for the person who makes fifty thousand dollars a year and lives in a $250,000 house.

You're broke, too. Your perception, and that of others, may be that you're a well-to-do homeowner. But the reality may be that you will find out who really owns the house if you miss a couple of mortgage payments.

Marketing gurus will tell you that *perception* is the deciding factor. Consumers buy a product based on what they perceive about it. There's little difference between a Toyota and a Lexus. They're made by the same company, same engineers, and workers using the same tools and the same machinery. The biggest difference is the label. It's the perception of the car that makes the big difference in the sales reports.

People are in miserable marriages because of the perception they had of the person they were dating and not the reality of the person's real character. The reality is, they really didn't get to know Ms. Pretty Eyes or Mr. Handsome before they said, "I do." Perception will escort you into situations that require no less than the hand of God to reach down and pull you out of them.

YOU CAN NEVER BE SUCCESSFUL LIVING LIFE
BASED ON PERCEPTION.

So, let's move into the *reality* lane on the freeway that leads to becoming who you were meant to be. If your reality is that you have a credit score of 500, and you live month to month and paycheck to paycheck, then own up to that fact so you know where you need to begin to change your situation. Don't compare yourself to others—especially those who are on social media trying to portray they have a fabulous life.

It's not their reality either! Most of them are crying themselves to sleep.

God can't help you until you reach your *reality zone*. I can't help you if you're not real with yourself. When you come to a point where you stop and admit that you're going to take responsibility for the decisions and the mistakes you've made, that's when you are getting real with yourself. You are who you are because of *you*, and you have what you have because of you.

There is nobody else to blame.

Perception is the way you see yourself—or the way others see you. Reality is the way God sees you. Stop lying to yourself about who you are. Stop believing what others say about you. Frankly, your opinion of yourself, or the way others see you, is not the most important thing. The most important opinion—the only one that can always be fully trusted to be true—is God's!

Everyone has shortcomings, but not many acknowledge them. When you ignore or deny your limitations or weaknesses, they grow and multiply. When you admit them and face them head on, you can overcome them. You won't be crying yourself to sleep anymore. You'll stop causing more debt, and your relationships will change. One of the biggest benefits of admitting and facing your shortcomings is that you'll be delivered from the opinions of other people.

Acknowledging your weaknesses frees your mind to seek the remedy. It may be hard to do because every motivational speaker tells you just the opposite.

"You're a lion, let me hear you roar!" they boast with fists waving in the air.

They don't want you to think about limitations, but I am telling you that you need to think about yours. Not only do I want you to think about them, I'm telling you to write them down so you can read them. It's a vital step in being able to get real with yourself.

STOP CHASING THE WRONG THINGS

I raised a lot of money with some friends in 2007 to invest in a project in the city of Jacksonville. The plan was to build nine hundred estate homes and sell them for one million dollars each.

All the preparation was completed. With due diligence, we purchased the land, had an appraisal, and paid for an environmental study. We then identified a bank that we thought would support our dream, and we asked them for the funding. They said they would give us a loan, and my friends and I were excited!

But a year passed, and we still hadn't closed on the loan. Then another year went by. The bank kept telling us that a recession was coming, and people were not going to be able to afford mortgages. To make a long story short, the banks and the government knew what was about to happen, but we had no idea. That was when the housing crash of 2008 happened. Since the bank never let us close on the loan, we lost about a million dollars.

I was so depressed that I spent three months in bed. That was a really dark time in my life. Then the Lord came to me and said, "I never told you to do it in the first place."

Wow! That's when I got *real* with myself. I was chasing the wrong things. I was chasing money and whatever made me feel good. I had to change my perspective. God never wanted me to chase money. I was supposed to be chasing my purpose. And getting real with myself is what got me out of my situation.

It's time for you to get real with yourself. Examine your motives. You don't have to compromise to be recognized.

ANYTHING YOU DO JUST FOR MONEY OR STATUS
WILL STRESS YOU OUT AND POSSIBLY LEAD
TO HEALTH PROBLEMS. EXAMINE YOUR MOTIVES. YOU
DON'T HAVE TO COMPROMISE TO BE RECOGNIZED.

I had to get real with myself. I was an insecure, adopted boy whose own birth mother didn't want. I felt I had something to prove to the world. Once I realized I didn't have to prove anything to anybody, my life changed. Some of you who are reading this book are trying to make an impression on people who don't even care about you.

Stop chasing the wrong things—like money, women, men, or tangible possessions. It may even be the approval or endorsement of someone in authority you are seeking. If so, know that if God approves you, that's what matters most. Be honest and do a self-examination. Time is of the essence, and I encourage you to use the balance of your days to chase after the things of God—like understanding, love, peace of mind, freedom, and education.

SHOW UP IN THE RIGHT PLACES

Everyone is assigned to do something, whether it's to be an entrepreneur, a mom, a wife, a motivational speaker, or an author. But that isn't what makes you stand out in a crowd. You become unique when you show up in the face of what you are called to do.

You can only be chosen when you decide to respond to God's call and show up, which means you can't be lazy. You can't expect success to just show up at your door. You must take the initiative to go out and show up where you need to be in order to begin to move toward your life's assignment. I'm challenging you to show up where you need to be as it relates to your calling.

My calling is to empower the world to be successful. I was chosen to help move people into where God wants them to be—to empower people with resources and relationships, to improve people's lives, to help grow their endeavors, and help develop their businesses.

I've especially been chosen to develop people into their divine assignment. To do that, I had to get over my insecurities with the sound of my small voice. I had to rise above my feelings about being abandoned at birth to show up and start my businesses, launch my ministries, and to do them exceptionally well.

I even had to fight through the fear of being transparent with my past and show up to write this book.

> THE CHOSEN ONES ARE THOSE
> WHO SHOW UP TO FULFILL THEIR CALLINGS.

CHAPTER INSPIRATION
GET REAL WITH YOURSELF

FIX YOUR THOUGHT LIFE

Your thoughts shape your future, and they precede everything you do. The thoughts in your mind exit your head by words from your mouth—then manifest in your life. Based on those thoughts, whatever has manifested can be good or bad.

- Have you ever done something that you wish hadn't happened?
- When you confided in someone about the event or situation, did they ask you, "What were you thinking?"

Fix your thoughts about yourself first, just as I had to do.

- What are you thinking about yourself?

Then fix your thoughts about other people, things, and situations.

- What are you thinking about those with whom you are in relationship?
- What are you thinking about your job situation?
- What are you thinking about your financial situation?
- Are your thoughts based on God's Word or the opinions of others?

CHANGE YOUR WORDS

Your words give instruction to produce life or death. Speak positive affirmations over your life on a daily basis. Call into existence those things you desire but do not presently see in the natural.

- What are you calling into existence in the life of your spouse?
- What are you calling into existence in the lives of your children?
- What are you calling into existence regarding your job?
- What are you calling into existence regarding your finances?

LISTEN TO YOUR OWN VOICE

Your voice is powerful—it matters. The first time I realized this fact about my own voice was when I was in the Army and men responded to a command I had given them. The revelation at that time was that I had a greater mission and assignment in life, and I later found out it was to help develop men.

- Your inner voice is commanding you to do what you were chosen to do. What is your inner voice commanding you to do?
- Listen intuitively and attentively.

MOVE FROM PERCEPTION TO REALITY

- Are you living a lifestyle you really can't afford?
- Do a reality check. Take responsibility for your circumstances by acknowledging your shortcomings, weaknesses, and mistakes. Move from the perception of how it appears, to the reality of what it really is.
- What is your real reality?

STOP CHASING THE WRONG THINGS

- Does your life revolve around the pursuit of money or tangible possessions? Does it revolve around seeking the approval of others?
- If so, *STOP*! You are inviting stress to take up residence in your body. My situation turned around when I started chasing after my purpose instead of money, things, and the approval of others.
- Focus on pursuing the things of God, and your life will change for the better.

SHOW UP IN THE RIGHT PLACES

The *chosen ones* are the individuals who show up to do the work they are called to do. Your gift can't make room for you if you're not using it. Show up and do it!

- If you have a talent to sing, are you showing up for choir at church?

- If you want to be in movies, are you positioning yourself to show up on a film set?
- If you want to start a business, have you showed up as an intern for a CEO to learn how to do it?

There are five words that will change your life and position you to be Chosen.

SHOW UP AND DO IT.

NOTES TO REMEMBER:

CHAPTER 2

NEVER STAY WHERE YOU'RE NOT VALUED

Are you in a relationship, church, or business where you are not being valued?

The first job I had after high school was working twelve hours a day as a busboy for a restaurant. It was a dirty job. I was making minimum wage, and I always felt like I wasn't moving up fast enough. I didn't feel valued. In the Army, I was always trying to help friends by giving them money and rides in my car. I rarely got a *thank you*. I felt like I was taken for granted.

The lesson I learned, as I stated it, was, "Never stay where I'm tolerated. Only go where I'm celebrated."

GO WHERE YOU ARE CELEBRATED, NOT TOLERATED

Many people stay in relationships, on jobs, or in places where they're just being tolerated, and that is no way to live! In most cases, when you stay where you are just being tolerated and not being valued, it's because *you* don't value *yourself.*

Without self-worth, nothing in yourself, your work, your relationships, or your faith will be worth anything!

IT IS IMPERATIVE THAT

YOU UNDERSTAND YOUR VALUE.

If you want to become the person you were meant to be, you're going to have to understand that you're invaluable! I believe what I'm providing through my ministries, my business, my books, my blogs, and my life is a valuable service. In fact, I believe it's so valuable that people should pay for it.

My belief about me is not arrogance. If people value what you have, then they should pay for it. If you're giving it away all the time, then maybe you don't value it.

Why does an iPhone cost $1,000? It's because Apple has inflated the perceived value of an iPhone so much in the minds of consumers that people are willing to pay $1,000 for that phone versus $100 for another phone that does the same thing. What's the difference in product value? The difference is not that one is better than the other. The difference is that one company *thinks it's more valuable* than the other.

So, how much do you value yourself?

A friend of mine once said:

Robert, the reason you only get $500 for a speaking engagement, and someone else gets $10,000 for the same speech that you gave, is because you're only charging $500, and they're charging $10,000. They think they're *worth* $10,000, and you think you're only worth $500. The difference is in the way you think. You don't think you're valuable enough. You don't think your story is valuable enough, your skill is valuable enough, or your experience is valuable enough to charge $10,000. So, you'll always be stuck at $500.

It wasn't until I started thinking that I was worth $10,000 as a speaker that people started paying for it.

You need to realize that corporate America will never pay you what you are worth. They're just not going to. When you go to them asking for a job, they're going to judge your resumé and say, "Well, you have ten years of experience, so we're going to pay you $50,000 a year. We're going to tell you when you can come to work and what you should wear. We're going to tell you where you can live, how many vacations you can take, and how much time off you can have. We don't care if you're sick or not. It doesn't really matter to us. We need you here. By the way, if you miss a day, we're taking it all away from you."

THE CHALLENGE IS TO FIND PEOPLE
WHO VALUE WHAT YOU HAVE TO OFFER.

You are of God, little children, and have overcome them, because He who is in you is greater than he who is in the world.

(1 John 4:4 NKJV)

I realize that everybody is not going to buy this book. Everybody is not going to invite Dr. Robert J. Watkins to their events or corporate functions. Everybody doesn't value me, and that's okay. I just need a few people who value me, who celebrate me, who are willing to pay for what I say, and for what I have to do. I have to diligently work hard to find those people and give them a million-dollars-worth of value, even though they may only have paid me $100.

There are people out there who will value what you have to say—or who will value your product or your service. You just have to locate them.

Twenty years ago when I first started *Kings and Priests*, no one wanted to talk about business or money. Even though they were financially broke and stressed out, had no savings, and had no retirement plan, people said I was a heretic.

Their thinking was that financial issues were worldly concerns that should be addressed outside of the church. I had to find a few people who would listen to what I had to say. It took ten years before anyone would listen to me. Like Jesus, I was rejected by those I wanted to help.

Jesus went to the eastern shore of the Sea of Galilee and delivered the man with the legion of demons. He helped that man like no one else could, and He was willing to help others. But the people in that region rejected Him.

> *And behold, the whole city came out to meet Jesus; and when they saw Him, they implored Him to leave their region.*
> (Matthew 8:34 NASB)

Even in His hometown of Nazareth, Jesus couldn't do a mighty work among them because of their unbelief.[5] Only a few people got healed. The rest of the people even tried to kill Him and throw Him off a cliff.

---

5 "And He could do no miracle there except that He laid His hands on a few sick people and healed them. And He wondered at their unbelief" (Mark 6:5-6).

He came to His own, and those who were His own did not receive Him. (John 1:11 NASB)

They got up and drove Him out of the city, and led Him to the brow of the hill on which their city had been built, in order to throw Him down the cliff. (Luke 4:29 NASB)

Jesus didn't stay where He wasn't valued. He went to the next city, where the multitudes showed up and many were healed. Jesus went from town to town, city to city, and village to village, where He was not only tolerated but also celebrated.

And when Jesus sent His disciples out on their own, He told them, *"If any household or town refuses to welcome you or listen to your message, shake its dust from your feet as you leave."* [6]

If you are in a place where you're not being valued, very few miracles can be done. Leave there so you can go where you will be welcomed, valued, and celebrated. Never stay where you're not valued—that's my mantra.

WHAT'S YOUR PVP
(PERSONAL VALUE PROPOSITION)?

In business, a *value proposition* is a promise of *value* to be delivered. It's the primary reason a prospect should buy from you. In life, you have to establish your value proposition. Why should people hire you, be your friend, buy your products, or marry you? What makes you special, different, and unique? You cannot allow other people to decide those things. That's your job.

In a nutshell, a value proposition is a clear statement that:

- Explains how you can improve their situation (relevancy).
- Delivers specific benefits to people (quantified value).

---

6   Matthew 10:14 NLT.

- Tells the people why they should buy from you and not from the competition (unique differentiation).

You have to present your value proposition as the first thing people see in your life. It should also be visible each and every time they meet you in person, on social media, or any other place.

RESPECT YOUR HEART'S INTELLIGENCE

Discern the agenda of other people's direction for your life, but find the courage to follow your own heart, and it will lead you to your chosen destiny.

Beware! Your heart must not always follow the crowd. You must be willing to stand alone as you follow God. Another person's opinion should never override your heart. Your heart is the birthplace for your increase or your decrease.

We read in the Word of God, in the book of Proverbs, *"Guard your heart above all else, for it determines the course of your life."* [7]

YOU MUST KEEP YOUR HEART IN GOOD SPIRITUAL
CONDITION, THEN IT WILL LEAD YOU TO YOUR
PROMOTION AND ADVANCEMENT.

My *heart* told me not to invest in that large land deal in Jacksonville, Florida, but my *head* was focused on the numbers and money. I moved forward with the negotiation because I was chasing the wrong thing, and I lost a lot of money and relationships in the process. I should have followed my heart.

---

7   Proverbs 4:23 NLT.

SURROUND YOURSELF
WITH DIVINE RELATIONSHIPS

You will meet people in life who are willing to walk with you, but that doesn't mean they are destined to be a part of your journey. It is critical to understand that *divine* relationships are there to help you follow your purpose. Many people are good, but they may not be good for your mission in life. And if they are not good for your mission in life, they will ultimately be a distraction.

I grew up with people and family who really didn't understand my mission. I had to find like-minded people who were moving in the same direction I was going. That is hard for a lot of individuals to do because they base their relationships on proximity, race, location, church affiliation, status, and so on.

You must seek out those who have similar goals and ambitions, and who are moving in the direction you are going—or those who have already achieved success in the field that you want to be in. You may not have anything else in common except a mission, but it will keep you accountable and motivated when those inevitable times come when you just don't *feel like it* or when you encounter discouraging situations or people.

If you examine a pack of animals, whether lions or deer, they surround themselves with others on the same mission. The lion's mission for the day is to find something to eat. The deer's mission for the day is to not be eaten. And they both are more successful when surrounded by others with the same agenda.

> YOU MUST SEEK OUT THOSE WHO HAVE THE SAME GOALS, AMBITIONS, ARE MOVING IN THE DIRECTION YOU ARE GOING, OR HAVE ALREADY ACHIEVED SUCCESS IN THE FIELD THAT YOU WANT TO BE IN.

GO BACK TO WHAT GOD ORIGINALLY TOLD YOU TO DO

Have you found yourself saying the following?

- "I'm not where I'm supposed to be."
- "I've spent too much money on this project."
- "I've spent too much time in this ministry or on this job."
- "I wasted a lot of time and energy being distracted."
- "I partied my life away."

I hear these complaints often from people and get asked for my advice about what to do to get out of the rut and into the fast lane toward becoming all they were meant to be. My advice is always, "Go back to what God originally told you to do. It's never too late. You're not too old or too broke. Go back to your original purpose and intent for your life."

And that's what I had to do for myself.

After I got out of the Army, I felt a call and a longing to help empower men who were struggling in their lives. I didn't know how to begin, because I had my own issues. So I joined a church, and I stayed there for about fifteen years. Over that time, I did nothing because I was afraid I would fail. I was afraid no one would support me or listen to me.

It reminded me of Moses when he stood before the burning bush and God gave him an assignment that was overwhelming. He had to go back to Egypt, the very place where a death warrant had been issued on his life. God told Moses to go and tell Pharaoh to let His people go. God wanted those men and women who were trapped in bondage to be released.

God chose Moses because he was the perfect person for the job, but Moses argued with God to try to get out of the assignment. For five years, I basically used the same arguments Moses did to argue with God about why I should not go.

- "Who am I?"
- "Who am I to go and help men by talking about their marriages, money issues, business issues, and issues with their children?"
- "Who am I to go and help these people?"

After all, I had my own issues.

But God wouldn't allow me to sleep. He wouldn't allow me to be successful in any other thing. This was something I had to do. It kept me up at night, and even when I did sleep, I dreamed about it. God constantly reminded me of my purpose. Not only that, other people started to sense I was not moving in the area where my purpose and my heart were leading me.

However, I stayed on my job, and I stayed in relationships that kept me average and feeling limited and paralyzed. But I couldn't blame any of those situations or people who brought me down. I had to blame myself and take responsibility for my non-action. There were no shackles on my feet. There were no handcuffs on my hands. There was no muzzle on my mouth. I was the only thing that was keeping me where I was not being valued.

Finally, I stepped out in faith and set up my first *Kings and Priests* meeting. I sent out invitations to about twenty men, and eight of them showed up in a golf course club house in Douglasville, Georgia. In the meeting I taught a John Maxwell message on leadership.

The guys loved it. I loved it. They had joy, and they had peace. And you know what? They wanted me to do it again! We had the same type of meeting the next month, and twenty men came. The next month, well over a hundred men came. We got so big that we had to move. We did our first quarterly meeting at the Ritz-Carlton in downtown Atlanta, where over 500 men came to hear what I had to say.

It grew from there, and in our last national meeting, we had over 8,000 people in attendance.

> I WOULD NOT BE IN THE PLACE
> WHERE I AM TODAY IF I HAD STAYED
> WHERE I WAS NOT VALUED.

If you are not yet sure what God created you to do, ask yourself the following questions. Your answers will lead you to your purpose.

- If I gave you a 100,000 square foot Walmart building, what would you do with it?
- If you go to the mall and see a teenage girl walking around pregnant, does that make you angry? Do unhealthy people sadden you? Does clutter get on your nerves? Does seeing the homeless strike a nerve?
- If you could teach three things to the next generation, what would you talk to them about?

The answers you gave to these questions should have convinced you there is something you're supposed to do. Do not let fear, people, or circumstances be your excuse for lack of action. The assignment and the purpose that's on your life may seem overwhelming. That's why you must walk by faith and not by sight.

The truth is, God has equipped you with the gifts and talents you need to accomplish the purpose He has specifically chosen for you. He is 100 percent for your success.

Some people do things so naturally that they don't even recognize they have a gift or talent that is being underutilized. Knowing your gifts and creating a vision for how to use them is important to becoming all you are meant to be.

Taking action is vital to your success. Don't be afraid because you're not a celebrity, or people don't know you. Your job is not to open a door; that's God's job. As long as you step out in faith and walk toward the doors, those doors will be opened. If a door doesn't open, you may be going in the wrong direction. Don't allow the word "No" to stop you from looking for another door. If you keep going, eventually you will get a "Yes."

> THE ONLY THING THAT CAN PREVENT YOU
> FROM GETTING TO WHERE YOU'RE SUPPOSED TO GO,
> AND KEEP YOU FROM BECOMING THE MAN
> OR WOMAN YOU ARE MEANT TO BE, IS YOU.

— CHAPTER INSPIRATION —
NEVER STAY WHERE YOU'RE NOT VALUED

GO WHERE YOU ARE CELEBRATED, NOT TOLERATED

If you are settling for a relationship, business, church, or job where you are not being valued, then give yourself permission to use the exit ramp.

You need to recognize that you have value. No one else will see your worth if you don't come to that conclusion about yourself. One way to do that is to find out what God says about you.

2 Timothy 1:7 says you are _____

Hebrews 13:21 says you are _____

Revelation 1:6 says you are _____

1 Corinthians 15:57 says you are _____

Matthew 5:3-14 says you are _____

Find the people and places that celebrate you—not just tolerate you—and your presence will be valued as a gift.

- Who or what is God telling you to exit out of?

Define Your PVP (*Personal Value Proposition*):

- What makes you relevant?
- What benefits does your life deliver to others?
- What makes you different from your peers?

RESPECT YOUR HEART'S INTELLIGENCE

Your heart is smart. Your heart is the birthplace for your increase—but can be the birthplace for your decrease, too. You must keep your heart in good spiritual condition in order for it to lead you to your promotion and advancement.

- What's in your heart that causes fear?
- Is there someone you need to forgive for hurting you in the past?
- What's in your heart that you haven't done yet?

SURROUND YOURSELF WITH
PEOPLE ON THE SAME MISSION

You must seek out those who have goals and ambitions, and who are moving in the direction you are going, or who have already achieved success in the field that you want to be in.

- One way to do this is to write out your personal Mission Statement.
- Then set goals to begin to achieve success.
- Include a projected time line for moving forward.
- Research those who have already achieved success in your field, and connect with them. Social media can help you connect even with those not in your immediate area.

GO BACK TO WHAT GOD ORIGINALLY TOLD YOU TO DO

I argued with God for about five years as to why I didn't think I should be chosen to empower men when I had my own issues. During that time, my life consisted of the mundane and average. It wasn't until I answered the call that I began to experience the supernatural happening in me, for me, and to me.

Do not let fear or excuses keep you from doing what you know God has told you to do.

- What excuses have kept you bound in fear?

God has qualified you even though you may feel inadequate.

- What gifts and talents do you have that are being underutilized?
- How can those gifts and talents help you achieve what God has told you to do?

> YOUR PROMOTION, INCREASE,
> AND PROVISION ARE WAITING FOR YOU
> AT THAT PLACE OF OBEDIENCE.

NOTES TO REMEMBER:

CHAPTER 3

TRANSITION TO THE NEXT LEVEL

It's time to move from comfort to courage.

Maybe as a young girl, you had a dream of this big fairy-tale wedding with thousands of people applauding you as you rode by in a beautiful white carriage. You envisioned yourself with beautiful shoes and a beautiful gown. Then as a teenage woman, you went to high school and some boy broke your heart.

Perhaps as a young boy, you imagined playing in the NFL or the NBA, and you were bigger than life. Then as a teenager, you went to high school and got injured after you made the team. Then your athletic ability declined.

Those childhood dreams consumed you even after someone or something popped your bubble. The big wedding didn't happen. The NBA didn't happen. If you continue holding on to that dream as you move into your twenties, thirties, and forties, you'll find yourself floundering through life. If you never get out of that initial dream stage, you will walk around resenting your spouse, resenting friends, and resenting your life. You will have a regret-filled spirit that you just can't seem to shake.

Maybe you grew up with the mindset of how others labeled you.

When I was growing up, there was a guy in the neighborhood named Jean. We called him *Jean-O the wino*. He was known by his alcoholism, so that's how he was branded. There was another guy in the neighborhood who used to ride the little yellow bus, and we called him *retarded*. I was known as the guy who was adopted.

People tend to define us by our issues or our weaknesses, so we grow up with the mindset of how others label us. This is the reason we need to reimagine our life to coincide with the thoughts that God has for us.

Where there is no vision, the people perish.

(Proverbs 29:18a KJV)

Right now, I want you to just reimagine your life. Write the vision down, detailing how you're going to spend the rest of your life. Set aside your memories; don't let the past determine or define your future. You will receive a larger vision; it should include making a difference in the lives of other people. If you think about it, all those former dreams were about how you could benefit yourself. Now start thinking about helping somewhere else and someone else.

DECIDE TO LIVE AGAIN

Have you experienced divorce or the death of a spouse? What about a failed business opportunity?

Most people who suffer some form of tragedy fall into a state of shock. That can be expected, and it isn't a problem when they recover and move forward with life. The problem arises when they stay in that state. We can choose to live again after a tragedy or loss.

> UNDERSTANDING THAT YOU HAVE A PURPOSE
> MEANS YOUR CIRCUMSTANCES ARE NOT
> BIGGER THAN YOUR GOD.

Even though you may experience a loss or failure, it doesn't mean that it is the end for you. Take your eyes off your own problem. Take your attention off yourself. I know that's hard to do, because it's easy to feel sorry for yourself.

> DETERMINE TO NOT LET SOCIETAL NORMS
> BECOME YOUR STANDARD. MAKE A DECISION TO
> REDEFINE WHAT LIVING MEANS TO YOU. ALLOWING
> YOURSELF TO LIVE AGAIN STARTS
> WITH THE DESIRE TO DO SO.

After my divorce, I was forced to find another way to live without the woman I was married to for twenty-two years. At that point in my life, I could have chosen to either be depressed about the past or happy about the future. It was my choice. While my life might have been imperfect, the one that thing that *was* perfect, divine, and constant was the fact that I was chosen for something greater. And that never changed.

You need to make the decision to live again after disappointment, failures, or things not going as planned. God is in the business of second, third, fourth, and forty chances to start over and get it right. Don't let the enemy keep you in a place of stagnation or fear.

Many people are merely existing. Existing, by definition, means to simply be present at the time. God doesn't want you to be simply present. He wants you to live! To live means to be in motion. You need to realize that regardless of what is going on in the present, you have a future that was predetermined by God before you were conceived.

Your future is far greater than your present circumstance.

Job was a man who suffered more than most of us. He lost his business, his wealth, his children, and his health. His friends accused him of bringing it all upon himself. His wife told him to curse God for everything and just give up. Job made a choice to remain steadfast in his faith and believed in the God he served. God rewarded Job's faith and perseverance in face of tribulation.

> So the Lord blessed Job in the second half of his life even more than in the beginning. Job lived 140 years after that, living to see four generations of his children and grandchildren.
>
> (Job 42:12, 16 NLT)

Deciding to live again sometimes means we need to hit the restart button. We may feel like we are already behind in life, and starting over will put us even further behind, but that couldn't be farther from the truth. Instead of trying to fix something that's broken, starting over can propel us ahead to become the best version of ourselves.

Here are seven things you may have to let go of or change when you decide to live again:

1. **Past Criticisms.** Sometimes we let what others say define us. Jean-O the wino had to let go of those past criticisms to move forward. I had to divorce myself from the opinions of other people. You have to let go of everyone else's expressions of disapproval of you or the things you have done. Let their judgment or analysis of you remain in their history book, not yours.

2. **Thinking You are Behind in Life.** There is nothing you can do about the past. Believe that you are where you are supposed to be—and that from this moment you are starting to do what you should be doing. When you get on the right track, God can supernaturally advance you beyond where you imagined you would be.

   "Yes indeed, it won't be long now." God's Decree.

   "Things are going to happen so fast your head will swim, one thing fast on the heels of the other. You won't be able to keep up. Everything will be happening at once—and everywhere you look, blessings! Blessings like wine pouring off the mountains and hills. I'll make everything right again for my people Israel." (Amos 9:13-14 MSG)

3. **Multi–Tasking.** Are you doing too much? Are you a *jack-of-all-trades* but a master of none? Sometimes we can't get one thing finished because we are working on five things all at once. Concentrate on completing the first thing before you move on to the second thing.

4. **Competing with Others.** You were created to do what only you can do. There is no competition when you are operating in your gift. If you are in *your* will for your life instead of God's will, then you will find yourself constantly comparing yourself to others.

5. **Trying to Get Rich at All Costs.** If your focus is on getting rich, you are compromising the important things in life such as family, friends, and relationships. Change your focus to your purpose, and you will be richer in the things that matter more than you can imagine.

6. **Waiting for Opportunities.** You must *create* opportunity—not *wait* for opportunity. Your gift can't make room for you if you are not using it.

7. **Relationships That Don't *Get You*.** Have you ever tried to force a person to like you? Isn't it draining? Remember that positive change for you may mean that some people from your past will not go with you into your future. The people who are assigned to you will gravitate toward you. You are not for everybody, so don't take it personally. You are fearfully and wonderfully made, and not everybody can handle who you are called to be. You are a divine design for those you are assigned to affect.

DON'T BE AFRAID TO START OVER WHEN
YOU MAKE THE DECISION TO LIVE AGAIN.

Your plan in starting over should involve making a difference somewhere by investing time in good causes. Try volunteering for a non-profit organization. Maybe you could go to the retirement community and talk to the elderly people or visit the bedridden in hospitals or nursing homes. They have so many stories to tell. It's a blessing for them to have a listening ear, and it's a blessing for the hearer as well.

My stepfather had diabetes, and because of that disease his right leg was amputated. He was practically bedridden for the last two years of his life. He was basically an atheist, and prior to his decline in health he wouldn't listen to any mention of Jesus or the Word of God.

When I was in college, I would visit him and read the Bible to him. I didn't know how much he looked forward to my visits until I went away for a summer and wasn't able to see him for a while. My stepmother told me he kept asking for me and wanted to know why I hadn't been around to read to him anymore. I was shocked. When my stepfather left this earth, he went on to be with the Lord.

START OVER—ACT AS THOUGH YOU HAVE NOTHING

Stripping yourself of worldly ideas and concepts is important since we all have the tendency to hang on to stuff that keeps us in bondage. I needed to release my mind from the bondage of things. I had to experience a season of lack in order to gain the right perspective on what was important.

Celebrate your life, not your possessions. When you're starting over with nothing, you have no reputation. Jesus said He wasn't trying to make himself famous. He came to do what the Father had purposed for His life. He put others ahead of himself, and that's what you should do as well.

A.W. Tozer in his essay, *Five Vows for Spiritual Power*, wrote, "Never own anything." Remember that what you possess, possesses you. Tozer wrote:

> I do not mean by this that you cannot have things. I mean that you ought to get delivered from this sense of possessing them. This sense of possessing is what hinders us. All babies are born with their fists clenched, and it seems to me it means: "This is mine!" That sense of "This is mine" is a very injurious thing to the spirit. If you can get rid of it so that you have no feeling of possessing anything, there will come a great sense of freedom and liberty into your life.
>
> Now don't think that you must sell all that you have and give it to charity. No, God will let you have your car and your business, your practice and your position, whatever it may be, provided you understand that it is not yours at all, but His, and all you are doing is just working for Him. You can be restful about it then, because we never need to worry about losing anything that belongs to someone else. If it is

yours, you're always looking in your hand to see if it's still there. If it's God's, you no longer need to worry about it.

Let me point out some things you'll have to turn over to God. Property is one thing. Some of the dear Lord's children are being held back because there's a ball and chain on their legs. If it's a man, it's his big car and fine home. If it's a woman, it's her china and her Louis XIV furniture and all the rest. Take that vase for instance. There it stands, and if anybody knocked it off and broke it the poor owner would probably lose five years from her life![8]

If you are seeking status and money, you may act fake and phony just to keep up appearances. Atlanta can be full of the *fake and the phony*. You don't know who is real and who is not. You don't know who really has it and who doesn't. I speak from experience because I was one of those people. I acted just like those fakers.

When I was around twenty-five years old, I realized my hairline was fading. Well, I was in corporate America, and I thought a black man with a bald head and goatee would look like a thug. I decided to do something about my fading hairline, so I bought a very expensive toupee. I had to grow my hair on the sides, then comb it so it kind of blended in.

It was windy and raining the first time I went to church wearing the toupee. I was feeling really good about myself. After the service, I went in the bathroom and looked at myself in the mirror. Guess what I saw? A crooked toupee that was about to fall off. I started crying right there in the bathroom. It was at that moment I realized I was in *people bondage.*

Many of us are living in lack because we are spending our money and time trying to please and impress other people.

8 http://www.neve-family.com/books/tozer/FiveVows.html

A couple of days after my toupee misadventure, I had the courage to shave my head. Whether or not I got compliments, I was getting comfortable with being who God created me to be. He meant for me to be a bald-headed man, and I think I'm doing pretty well with it.

LAUGH, BREATHE, AND LOVE AGAIN

Years later, I was in St. Louis ministering at a church and talking about how to get rid of *people bondage.* I told the toupee story. It wasn't meant to be funny, but everyone was cracking up laughing. Thinking about the fact that I actually had on a toupee before I was thirty years old, I couldn't help but join them in the laughter. It's true that laughter works like medicine.[9]

Just because you are chosen for a great work doesn't mean you are not going to make mistakes or find yourself in desperate situations. It does mean that God's hand is on your life and that grace is following you to protect you. When you find yourself in troubling times, sometimes you just have to laugh.

Laughter is a powerful antidote to stress, pain, and conflict. Nothing works faster or more dependably to bring your mind and body back into balance than a good laugh. Humor lightens your burdens, inspires hopes, connects you to others, and keeps you grounded, focused, and alert. It also helps you to release anger and be more forgiving.

With so much power to heal and renew, the ability to laugh easily and frequently is a tremendous resource for surmounting problems, enhancing your relationships, and supporting both physical and emotional health. Best of all, this priceless medicine is fun, free, and easy to use.

---

9   "A merry heart does good, like medicine, but a broken spirit dries the bones" (Proverbs 17:22 NKJV).

Here are seven benefits of laughter:

1. Laughter relaxes the whole body. A good, hearty laugh relieves physical tension and stress, leaving your muscles relaxed for up to 45 minutes after.
2. Laughter boosts the immune system. Laughter decreases stress hormones and increases immune cells and infection-fighting antibodies, thus improving your resistance to disease.
3. Laughter triggers the release of endorphins, the body's natural feel-good chemicals. Endorphins promote an overall sense of well-being and can even temporarily relieve pain.
4. Laughter protects the heart. Laughter improves the function of blood vessels and increases blood flow, which can help protect you against a heart attack and other cardiovascular problems.
5. Laughter burns calories. It's no replacement for going to the gym, but one study found that laughing for 10 to 15 minutes a day can burn about 40 calories—which could be enough to help you lose three or four pounds over the course of a year.
6. Laughter lightens anger's heavy load. Nothing diffuses anger and conflict faster than a shared laugh. Looking at the funny side can put problems into perspective and enable you to move on from confrontations without holding onto bitterness or resentment.
7. **Laughter may even help you to live longer.** A study in Norway found that people with a strong sense of humor outlived those who don't laugh as much. The difference was particularly notable for those battling cancer.[10]

---

10 Excerpts from https://www.helpguide.org/articles/mental-health/ laughter-is-the-best-medicine.htm

> DON'T WALK AROUND LIFE
> BEING HATEFUL, MEAN, AND SPITEFUL.
> INSTEAD, USE THE GIFT OF LAUGHTER.

BREATHE

When you take a deep breath, it sets the tone for relaxation. It will help you keep your sanity and manage stress. Deep breathing has its health benefits just as laughter does.

- It relaxes your muscles.
- Oxygen gets to your cells.
- Increases system functionality.
- Lowers your blood pressure.
- Improves detoxification.[11]

LOVE

Love is undeniably a good feeling, and humans are wired for connection. The right kind of love is proven to improve our health physically, spiritually, socially, and mentally. When we cultivate good relationships, we receive a harvest of rewards.

I'm not limiting this to romantic love, because love perks extend to other close relationships such as with a friend, relative, or parent. The key is to feel connected, respected, and valued by other people—and to feel a sense of belonging.

I had to give myself permission to love again. God is giving you permission to love again, too. Don't let the divorce or death of someone you loved keep you in *lonely-bondage*. Everyone recovers differently, and not in the same time span. The bottom line is that we must decide to recover and not remain stuck. You may even

---

11 www.livestrong.com Lung Health

have to first learn how to love people again—and especially those who have hurt you.

Here are five things you have to release so you can love again correctly:

1. **Doubt.** Being wounded can leave you doubtful that you are worthy of being loved or finding someone to love—or even doubtful that you want to attempt it again.

2. **Emotional Decisions.** Don't be needy or desperate because you are lonely. This may cause you to connect with the wrong person, which is worse than being alone.

3. **Controlling Every Situation.** When a relationship hasn't worked out well, you may have said, "That won't happen again!" You become controlling in order for you to assure yourself that you won't experience disappointment, pain or hurt again. This is not going to work out to your advantage. Recognize it and release it.

4. **Undervaluing Yourself.** When you don't recognize your value, you will settle for average or mediocre, instead of greatness and the supernatural. In fact, you are slapping God in the face when you minimize the value of His creation called *you*.

5. **Fear.** Perfect love casts out all fear. God has not given us a spirit of fear, but one of power, love, and a sound mind.[12] Remember that you have nothing to fear, nothing to hide, and nothing to lose.

Whatever you sow, you shall also reap.[13] Practice sowing love to your friends and neighbors, and even to the difficult-to-love individuals. Jesus is our example of how to love difficult people.

---

12 2 Timothy 1:7.
13 Galatians 6:7.

TAKE THE LEAP

Getting to the next level begins with defining what the next level is for you. Taking the leap is about accepting the risk in doing whatever you need to do to transition to the next level.

It's going to require faith and courage to start a new business, to walk away from a toxic relationship, or to start a ministry that no one said you should do—or that no leader endorsed you to move forward in. You're going to have to know within your heart that this is what you're supposed to do.

You must believe that God led you to that cliff. I advise people to take the risk and jump.

One of the things you can do to help shift your mindset is to literally jump, dance, and run.

Steve Harvey wrote a book titled, *Jump*.[14] In it, he says, "Just do it." However, it is important that you make sure you are leaping into the right pond.

When you are ready to leap, do you have a plan B? That was a trick question, because if you have a Plan B, then you shouldn't leap. Real success requires no Plan B. If you're getting married to someone, and you believe you should be with them "till death do us part," you don't have a Plan B. If you have a Plan B, then Plan A is probably not going to work out, because you're always going to keep Plan B in the back of your mind.

You can decide to put it all on the line. If you don't take the leap, that means you're spending your life standing on that cliff just wishing and hoping. You will never really know or experience the destiny that's waiting for you until you take the leap.

Theodore Roosevelt wrote in *Strenuous Life*:

> Far better it is to dare mighty things, to win glorious triumphs, even though checkered by failure, than to take

---

14 *Jump: Take the Leap of Faith to Achieve Your Life of Abundance*, by Steve Harvey, published by Amistad, 2017.

rank with those poor spirits who neither enjoy much nor suffer much, because they live in the gray twilight that knows neither victory nor defeat.[15]

GET OUT OF YOUR COMFORT ZONE

Are you comfortable? Comfort is necessary when you are looking for the right chair for your *man cave*, or the right mattress for your bed. However, the danger of staying in your comfort zone when it comes to walking in the life God wants you to have is that nothing special happens there.

Your comfort zone is not the space where uniqueness lives. It is also possible that your presence there—the reason you remain there—is because you are subconsciously trying to imitate someone else. That's certainly not going to work out well for you. You were fearfully and wonderfully created,[16] and God doesn't duplicate molds. So be the authentic person you were created to be.

Maybe you're at the factory job where you were hired when you graduated from high school. You've been working the same job month after month, and year after year. Do you think you should work to just pay bills and then die? That's why you're tired of spending your life on that merry-go-round—because it's not rewarding. You're ready to get off, but your comfort zone is keeping you there.

That type of living is what I call the *permissive* will of God. It's what God allows, but you're not fulfilling your purpose. You're not fulfilling what you were born to do, but you're scared to get out of the boat. You're just working for money or because somebody told you that's what you should be doing. Either way, your destiny is waiting, but you're stuck on autopilot.

15 *The Strenuous Life: Essays and Addresses*, by Theodore Roosevelt, published by Dover Publications, Inc., 1901, page 2.
16 Psalm 139:14.

To move out of autopilot-mode, you must acknowledge what's been holding you back. If you're not in good health, is it because you smoke, drink, don't get enough sleep, or eat too much? Is it procrastination that's keeping you stuck on autopilot? Do you need to start saying "No" to things, certain people, invitations, or toxic relationships?

Successful people understand how to say "No" and set boundaries, because they're protecting the most valuable thing in their life—their time. If you're a person who doesn't like offending people, then having to decline someone is probably out of your comfort zone.

Once you have identified what's been holding you back and keeping you in your comfort zone, you need to start making small steps toward your *courage zone.*

Personally, I didn't want to be in business or ministry, I just wanted to work a job. I had a corner office, an assistant, and staff. From the outside looking in, it appeared that I was doing well, but I wasn't happy at all. In fact, I was basically depressed.

Money makes you comfortable—not happy. I was joyless. My life was on autopilot.

So, what do you do once you recognize you are operating on autopilot? The first thing that I had to do was write a business plan. That's why I started *Conquer Consulting*—to help people put a plan in place to get them out of their comfort zones. Once you put your plan in writing, then you can walk toward the future you desire.

For me to leave my job, I had to have a plan. And that plan put me on the course to where I am today. Without the plan, I'd still be stuck living in my comfort zone.

Moving toward your courage zone also means identifying the fear that has been trying to hold you back. You may fear what people are going to say, fear failing, fear going broke, or fear losing everything.

The opposite of courage is fear.

Perhaps Joshua felt fear and apprehension when his mentor Moses died, when God spoke to him and told him to be strong and courageous. He had three million people he was called to lead into Canaan, the Promised Land.

> *Have I not commanded you? Be strong and of good courage; do not be afraid, nor be dismayed, for the Lord your God is with you wherever you go.* (Joshua 1:9 NKJV)

Well, there's a promised land that God has for you. That's where your money, the love of your life, your good health, your business, and your ministry are waiting for you. God wants you to take those steps toward your promised land. He told Joshua to have courage, and that's what I'm telling you to do. After all, you're backed by God.

> *Be strong and of good courage, do not fear nor be afraid of them; for the Lord your God, He is the One who goes with you. He will not leave you nor forsake you.*
>
> (Deuteronomy 31:6 NKJV)

Now that you're out of your comfort zone, here are the five stages from transition to transformation:

1. **Pregnant Stage.** You are pregnant with a vision or an idea from God about your life, business, ministry, and family. It's time to birth your vision.

2. **Purging Stage.** Anyone who is successful and full of life-lessons has experienced this stage. This is a difficult stage because things and people begin to exit your life as you change and are becoming more intent on birthing your vision. If God is allowing people or material possessions to exit your life, He will make sure that new things enter your life. It may be a dry season before the newness appears, but

that's alright. You may even feel like you are not going to make it, but rest assured, you're going *through* the purging stage, you're *not staying* there.

3. **Process Stage.** God is now beginning to give you the plan and the strategy to succeed. The same God who gave you the vision will give you the process. He did the same thing with Noah. You need a plan, and you need to get it from God. You don't need to get it from Wall Street or the bank.

4. **Placement Stage.** You are now where *God wants* you to be—not where *you want* to be. Your education may have gotten you to this point, but now you are in the place where your gifts and talents can be used. That means you have left His *permissive* will and now you're in His *perfect* will. The safest place to be is in God's perfect will for your life.

5. **Pursue Stage.** You're in motion now, and relationships and resources are attracted to you. You don't have to chase people anymore, now they're tracking you down.

After going through these stages, you've added value to a lot of people's lives, and now you are happy, fulfilled, and satisfied. You have transitioned, and now you are pursuing it with all your heart. Your life has transformed along with those who are following you. You will also be encouraging those who are watching from afar.

CHAPTER INSPIRATION
TRANSITION TO THE NEXT LEVEL

DECIDE TO LIVE AGAIN

Most people who suffer some form of tragedy fall into a state of shock. However, you can choose to live again after a tragedy or loss. Understanding that you have purpose means your circumstances are not bigger than your God.

- Does this describe you?
- You must *decide* to get up, dust off your knees, and *continue* on with your life.
- Stop *existing* and start *living*.
- What is your first step toward living instead of just existing?

START OVER—ACT AS THOUGH YOU HAVE NOTHING

Strip yourself of worldly perceptions and notions, and stop trying to keep up with appearances.

- Release yourself from the bondage of material possessions.
- Starting over can be better than trying to force broken pieces together.
- What are you stripping out of your life so you can have a clean start?

LAUGH, BREATHE, AND LOVE AGAIN

There are physical, emotional, mental, and health benefits attached to laughter and deep breathing exercises.

- Watch a comedy movie.
- Take a deep breath, relax, and take another deep breath.
- Give yourself permission to love again.
- God is the author of love, and He has written it in your story.

TAKE THE LEAP

What have you wanted to do before you bought into the lie of an insecure family member or *friend* telling you that you couldn't do it?

- Taking the leap is just about accepting the risk involved in doing whatever you need to do to transition to the next level.
- Leap, and the net will appear.

GET OUT OF YOUR COMFORT ZONE

To walk into the life God wants you to have, it is necessary to leave your comfort zone and enter your courage zone.

- The prerequisite for entering your chosen assignment is not comfort, it's obedience, and that takes courage.
- What is God asking you to do?

NOTES TO REMEMBER:

CHAPTER 4

CHANGE WHERE YOU LIVE

Have a mind that matters.

When I say change where you live, I'm not suggesting that you relocate to another state or look for a new residence. I want you to locate where your *state of mind* is relative to how you process information.

Reading is a good exercise because you can live vicariously in places where you can't live physically. You have the power to transport yourself to wherever you want to be—living the life you want to live through meditation. You must be able to visualize it before you can experience it. If you can't imagine yourself living in that house, or recording that song, or writing that book, or running that business, then it's not going to happen.

I want you to change the address in your mind from *Barely Making It Avenue* to *Overflow Way.*

Wherever you allow your mind to travel, that's where you'll go. To change where you live means to change your mindset. If you have a wealthy mindset, you're going to say and do things that wealthy people do. The same goes for having a POOR mindset which means you will *Pass Over Opportunities Repeatedly*, and unfavorable results will manifest.

THROW OUT THE POISON

Poison is defined as something that is destructive or harmful, or something that inhibits the course of a reaction or process.[17] Many times when you mention the word *poison*, people relate it to serious matters such as drug abuse. However, your poison could be so hidden in your daily life that you don't even recognize it as being the thing that is harmful to you and keeping you from becoming the person you were meant to be.

Your poison could be as simple as procrastination, the love of money, jealousy, or wasting too much time on social media. Whatever is holding you back is considered poisonous to your destiny.

One of the things that was impeding my progress in regards to my Kings and Priests ministry was the fear of being responsible for somebody else's life. I was running away from it, but God was calling me to it.

I can also say that money was a past poison for me. Money is not evil; it's the *love of money* that's evil.[18] Yes, we need money, but the pursuit of it can be obsessive and addictive. In my early days, I thought money was the cure for everything that was wrong in my life. I reasoned that if I had money I could change my circumstances, and that in turn would change how I was feeling on the inside. For me, that wasn't true.

17 https://www.merriam-webster.com/dictionary/poison
18 "For the love of money is a root of all kinds of evil. Some people, eager for money, have wandered from the faith and pierced themselves with many griefs" (1 Timothy 6:10).

I eventually put money ahead of relationships. I missed a lot of time at home because my priorities were out of alignment. Money had a hold on me instead of it being the other way around. But eventually, I was freed from the bondage of the money trap and was able to move forward with what God was calling me to do with my life.

> YOU MUST IDENTIFY WHATEVER IS HOLDING UP YOUR PROGRESS AND MAKE THE SHIFT EITHER PHYSICALLY OR MENTALLY TO GET FREE FROM ITS GRASP.

You must also be mindful of the company you keep so that someone else's poison doesn't become yours. For example, if one of your friends struggles with pornography, drinking, gluttony, or fornication, being in their company when they are indulging is not good for your focus. Energy is transferable, and so are poisons.

GET RID OF EMOTIONAL TRIGGERS

Don't go to the grocery store when you're hungry, because you will overspend and purchase every item that you have ever enjoyed eating in your life. You must start making right decisions and not emotional decisions.

Your feelings lie! Don't make a decision when you're angry, sad, or even happy. People make life-changing decisions—such as getting married—based on emotional experiences. Words spoken in anger can't be recalled, so the damage resurfaces even years later. You can let a trigger cause you to give your tongue permission to fire off emotional bullets that scathes the ears of all the listeners.

We have all seen stories in the news or on social media where someone gets in a fit of rage and makes a split-second decision that changes the course of their lives forever. If they had just been able to control their emotions, the results would have had a higher chance of working in their favor.

- What are your emotional triggers?
- Do you get angry at the thought of an old boyfriend or girlfriend?
- Do you want to eat everything in your path when a sad event happens?
- Do you want to test drive a new car every time you go past a dealership?
- Do you feel heat rising to the top of your head as soon as your co-worker or boss comes close to your cubicle?
- Do you get emotionally affected by someone posting something negative about you on social media?

You need to know what your triggers are and remind yourself that you are committed to a goal or person. Doing so will help you avoid making emotional decisions that compromise your goals and cause you to forfeit the success you are working toward obtaining.

ASK FOR HELP FROM THE RIGHT RESOURCES

How come men don't like asking for directions when they're driving and then get lost?

Pride is a major factor why people stay stuck in their circumstances. You have to change where you mentally live. Sometimes that means you need to get help from those who are qualified to help you. Divine directions will put you on the right course and save you from having to turn around, take detours, and arrive later than expected. Don't let your pride hold you hostage any longer.

> *Pride goes before destruction, and a haughty spirit before a fall.* (Proverbs 16:18 NKJV)

Seek the help you need, whether it's clinical counseling or professional consulting. When you are on your way to becoming who you were meant to be, you need a coach. I have mentors, and you should, too. A mentor doesn't have to be someone you can touch or feel. In this digital world that we live in today, a virtual mentor can be just as beneficial.

I am chosen to be a financial deliverer and to help the chosen ones discover and fulfill their destiny. I accomplish that through my ministry, Kings and Priests, and through my business, Conquer Worldwide. Conquer Worldwide has a consulting arm called Conquer Consulting. We have been successful in helping other ministries and businesses get started, develop, and become prosperous through our consulting service. You need a strategy, and we can help you.[19]

It is wise to get help from the *right* resources, not just any resource. Choosing the wrong resource will delay your productivity. Don't seek advice from someone not qualified to assist you.

But how do you choose the right resource?

You observe the people or businesses, examine their fruit, and determine if their expertise can help you on your mission. Referrals are backed by someone who has tried the service or product. Therefore, their opinions may help you determine if they are a viable resource.

Most importantly, do not forget the resource called *you*. You are your most valuable resource.

Delicately interwoven into the fabrics that make up *you* is a tag that says you were not made in the USA or any other country.

---

19 https://www.conquerworldwide.com/

They were handcrafted by the maker of life, and you were *chosen* for such a time as this.

Everything starts with your desire. You already have everything within you that's required for you to advance in the Kingdom.

MIND YOUR OWN BUSINESS

PLEASE, I BESEECH THEE

TO MIND YOUR OWN BUSINESS.

The above statement is a double entendre, and I will not back-pedal from your first thought. Yes, I literally mean to mind your own business.

How can you be effective concerning your own matters if your nose is meddling in someone else's affairs? Perhaps a gossiping spirit is hindering your progress, and besides, it's not pleasing to God. Minding your own personal business helps you to stay focused, have clarity about your mission, and remain on target to hit *your* destiny bull's-eye.

That you also aspire to lead a quiet life, to mind your own business, and to work with your own hands, as we commanded you, that you may walk properly toward those who are outside, and that you may lack nothing.

(1 Thessalonians 4:11-12 NKJV)

Now, let's talk about minding your own professional business. Whatever you discover that you are chosen to do, handle it as if you're operating a physical brick-and-mortar business, whether it's incorporated or not. You are the CEO of *you*. Successful CEO's follow routines, count the costs, plan, strategize, and set goals. They are doing something on a consistent basis that is producing desired results. Your daily habits are creating your future.

What habits to do you need to delete, modify or adopt in order to be productive?

Some of you are self-sabotaging your success by sleeping too much, watching excessive TV, overindulging in social media, or engaging in too many other non-income-producing activities. Take inventory of your time. Millionaires and billionaires will agree that the hours on the clock are their most precious commodity. We all have the same hours, minutes, and seconds in a day. The difference is what we chose to do with them.

A typical day for me begins with prayer, followed by exercise, then to my office. I have a physical office, but if you do not have one, there are plenty of virtual locations to use as somewhere to report to when conducting your business. The goal is to adapt a CEO mindset, and you will see major progress in accomplishing your chosen task.

Here are three tips on how to incorporate a CEO mindset:

1. **Plan your day.** You either fail to plan or plan to fail. Start planning a day at a time, then you can graduate to planning weeks and months.
2. **Stick to a schedule.** Develop a morning routine or evening routine to launch you into CEO mode. It has been articulated that doing something for twenty-one days creates a habit.
3. **Develop a spirit of excellence.** Do what you say; say what you mean; and mean what you say. Be the CEO who operates with integrity. Thinking short term and taking short cuts will lead to pre-mature death of your vision.

For those who know they have been assigned to start a business and to leave a business behind them for generational wealth, it's very important for you to understand how to think like a CEO. A Chief Executive Officer is a leader, and there is a difference between being a manager and being a leader. A leader is someone who has vision. A leader leads and directs people. A manager leads things, systems, and operations. As a visionary, you have to lead your followers with a clear and definitive vision.

> *Where there is no vision, the people perish: but he that keepeth the law, happy is he.* (Proverbs 29:18 KJV)

The people who will follow you are motivated by your passion and leadership. If you don't have a clear vision, you will lose followers, or they will limit their duties to performing the basic job description. They definitely will not go above and beyond the call of duty.

The most valuable part of your organization is not money, it is people. It doesn't matter what industry you're in, you must understand that you are *first* in the people business. You must learn how to work with and develop people. The CEO understands that teamwork makes the dream work, and he keeps others in mind as he plans out the manifestation of the vision.

You should have at least a twenty-year plan for your business. Super CEOs have a forty-year vision for their business. Do your research to understand your industry and the different trends that may affect your bottom-line so you become an expert. After all, you are the leader, and if anyone should be the expert, it should be you.

GAIN CONFIDENCE IN *YOU*

Do you find that one of the stumbling blocks to your success *is your lack of self-confidence?*

You are not alone. So many dreams are in a holding pattern because the dreamer is scared. Perhaps the fear of failure has paralyzed you to the point that you start talking yourself out of attempting to do the thing that has been in your heart for years. Guess what? That longing you have is not going anywhere, so why not position yourself to win? It starts with you getting a *confidence booster* in your spirit.

Have you ever watched a singer onstage at a concert? There is always another person on the stage with the main artist who is known as the *hype guy*. The hype guy's job is to be the sidekick to the artists and accompany them on stage with the purpose of getting the crowd excited. Their presence even encourages the artists to turn their performance up a notch.

When you are in the beginning stages of discovering what you are chosen to do and gaining the confidence to do it, you will most likely have to be your own hype person. Be excited about your own vision first. If you are lackluster in your posture concerning what you believe you are called to do, you will not attract the resources you need to accomplish the task.

In *The Confidence Solution*, Dr. Keith Johnson writes:

> Confidence is the bridge between where you are and where you want to be. . . . It does not matter how successful you are at this moment, deep down inside you know there's a higher level of achievement for your personal and business life. When you stop reaching higher, you start sliding backwards toward fear, uncertainty and doubt (FUD) . . . The gap between where you are and where you want to be will always demand a new level of confidence. If you are continually stretching yourself to maximize your full potential, you should never feel satisfied, content or comfortable. Satisfaction and contentment with your current level of success kills your potential. When you get to the place where you are content with your latest accomplishments, you put yourself into a box of containment that keeps you from progressing to the next level.[20]

20 Johnson, Keith. *The Confidence Solution* (Viking Penguin, 2011) excerpts from chapter "The Crisis of Confidence."

How do you gain confidence? Here are four ways:

1. **Be certain that what you are striving for is not against the will of God.** This will give you a *God-fidence*, a godly confidence, which will sustain and encourage you in a divine manner.

   And this is the confidence that we have toward him, that if we ask anything according to his will he hears us. (1 John 5:14 ESV)

2. **Cancel doubt and unbelief *conversations*.** These conversations can start in your own mind or can be from outsiders. Speak life over your vision and exercise *faith-talk*.

3. **Associate with other dreamers.** This will help you to stay motivated.

4. **Plan how to get it done.** When you schedule and plan out your vision, you can see how it will manifest. This will most assuredly boost your confidence.

Gaining confidence also has to do with how you view yourself. You are important. When you see yourself as God sees you, this will produce a confident countenance. Your motives and actions may be misjudged by family and friends, but you must not be discouraged. You are your own cheerleader and mascot first. Confidence produces positive energy, and energy is contagious. Remind yourself of God's thoughts about you.

"For I know the thoughts that I think toward you," says the Lord, "thoughts of peace and not of evil, to give you a future and a hope." (Jeremiah 29:11 NKJV)

Being confident of this very thing, that He who has begun a good work in you will complete it until the day of Jesus Christ. (Philippians 1:6 NKJV)

Be confident that God has begun a good work in you! His Word says He will complete it. God doesn't lie. That should be all you need for a confidence booster.

> THINGS WILL START TO ALIGN
> AND WORK IN YOUR FAVOR WHEN YOUR
> CONFIDENCE KICKS INTO OVERDRIVE.

BE CONSISTENT

Consistency is the key to your breakthrough, whether it's in relationships or professional endeavors. This is an area where I have struggled, myself. If you're not consistent, you won't get results.

Consider the examples of Olympic gold medalists. They did not just happen to wake up and get selected to be included in a group of world-class athletes. To make that prestigious list required years of *consistent* training, sacrifices, and discipline. They stayed focused and determined to reach the goal of being included in the epitome of athletic competitions, which only comes around every four years.

Consider yourself in training like an Olympian because you, too, are chosen to be a winner.

> IF YOU'RE NOT CONSISTENT,
> YOU WON'T GET RESULTS.

Here are five steps to help you become more consistent:
1. **Keep your eye on your *why*.** Your "why" is your reason for doing what you do. My reason for writing this book and being a wealth builder is because I want to help others. You have to define your *why*. Is it to help your family, children,

community, or ministry? Whatever it is, you have to be relentless in keeping your *why* in your front-view mirror.

2. **Choose one thing and stick to it.** Psychologists say you shouldn't do two major things at the same time. For example, don't try to stop smoking and stop eating sweets simultaneously. This is hard for the multi-taskers, but normally something will suffer from lack of proper attention, and you may not get results in one of those areas. Wait until you achieve results from concentrated efforts toward one goal before you move on to the next one.

3. **Schedule your priorities.** Determine what your priorities are, and don't let anything be an interruption. Schedule time with your spouse, children, and to do ministry. If you are having financial challenges, you may even need to schedule time to make a savings deposit. When your life is out of balance, that opens the door for you to be pulled in many directions, then productive activities get reduced to a minimum.

4. **Ignore your feelings.** There will be times when you just don't *feel like it.* You need to ignore what your feelings may be telling you. Napoleon Hill wrote a book called the *The Master Key to Riches.* He said, "The great master key to riches is nothing more or less than the self-discipline necessary to help you take full and complete possession of your own mind."[21] Self-discipline is the ability to make yourself do what you should do, when you should do it, whether you feel like it or not. Make a written plan, organize the plan, set priorities and do something every day until you're successful.

5. **Don't beat yourself up.** If you miss the mark, encourage yourself to pick up where you left off. You may have missed an opportunity or not taken full advantage of a business

21 From *The Master Key to Riches*, by Napoleon Hill, published by tarcherperigee, 2007, page 290.

relationship, but new mercies come every morning. Extend yourself a *grace card* and get back on track.

— CHAPTER INSPIRATION —
CHANGE WHERE YOU LIVE

THROW OUT THE POISON
I define poison as something that is destructive or harmful, or that which inhibits a process.

- What is interfering with your process?
- Is it the love of money, an unhealthy relationship, or another type of addictive behavior?
- Define what your poison is and get free from its grasp. You have to locate the address of your mind and change the street it lives on.

GET RID OF EMOTIONAL TRIGGERS
Don't make decisions when you are angry, sad, or even happy.

- What person or situation causes a shift in your emotional state?
- Do you get angry at the thought of an old boyfriend or girlfriend?
- Do you want to eat everything in your path when a sad event happens?
- Do you want to test drive a new car every time you go past a dealership?
- Do you feel heat rising to the top of your head as soon as your co-worker or boss comes close to your cubicle?
- Do you get emotionally affected by someone posting something negative about you on social media?

ASK FOR HELP FROM THE RIGHT RESOURCES

Pride is a major factor of why people stay stuck in their circumstances.

- Does pride keep you from asking for help?
- Divine directions will put you on the right course and save you from having to turn around, take detours, and arrive later than expected.
- There are professional and clinical resources that are qualified to assist you, and Conquer Worldwide is one of them.

MIND YOUR OWN BUSINESS

How can you be effective concerning your own matters if your nose is meddling in someone else's affairs?

- Is a gossiping spirit hindering your progress?
- Successful CEOs follow routines, count the costs, plan, strategize, and set goals. They are doing something on a consistent basis that is producing desired results.
- What habits to do you need to delete, modify, or adopt in order to be productive?

GAIN CONFIDENCE IN *YOU*

So many dreams are in a holding pattern because the dreamer is scared.

- Has the fear of failure paralyzed you to the point that you are talking yourself out of attempting to do the thing that has been in your heart for years?
- It starts with you getting a *confidence booster* in your spirit. Be confident that our God has begun a good work in you!

His word says He will complete it, and our God doesn't lie.
- Things will start to align and work in your favor when your confidence kicks into overdrive.

BE CONSISTENT

Consistency is the key to your breakthrough, whether it's in relationships or professional endeavors. If you're not consistent, you won't get results.

- In what areas do you need to be more consistent in moving toward becoming the person you are called to be?
- How are you going to improve your consistency in those areas?

NOTES TO REMEMBER:

CHAPTER 5

CHOOSE THE RIGHT PEOPLE

Teamwork makes the dream work.

Having the right team is critical for you to successfully reach your destination of becoming who you were created to be. No man is an island, and no person with a marginal amount of success has accomplished it alone.

Choosing the wrong people to have in your life professionally or personally will cause a detour, delay, or destruction of the plan God has for you. Choosing the right people will minimize stress, strain, and struggle on your pathway to success.

There are individuals assigned to your life, and you will know them by their fruit. Consider those who adjust their schedules to accommodate you in a time of need, those who protect your reputation, those who practice confidentiality and won't use information to hurt you, and those who challenge you. These people will either start with you, or you will attract them along the way.

Your gift will make room for you and bring you into the presence of great people.

Great people have character—integrity, honesty, humility, emotional intelligence, mental intelligence, and trustworthiness. I could list a number of other character traits—most of them rooted in what Scripture describes as the fruit of the Spirit.

The Message talks about the character of the right people:

> *But what happens when we live God's way? He brings gifts [character traits] into our lives, much the same way that fruit appears in an orchard—things like affection for others, exuberance about life, serenity. We develop a willingness to stick with things, a sense of compassion in the heart, and a conviction that a basic holiness permeates things and people. We find ourselves involved in loyal commitments, not needing to force our way in life, able to marshal and direct our energies wisely.*
>
> (Galatians 5:22-23 MSG)

I have assembled an awesome team of people to help me. You also should look for wealth-building personalities when you are choosing others to help you bring your vision to manifestation. I am going to use real-life examples of people in this explanation of six wealth-building personalities—and by the way, they're all billionaires. If they can do it, why can't you? Pay attention, because you are going to see yourself in one or more of these personalities.

THE INNOVATOR

People known as *creators* are visionaries. They see the big picture. However, they're usually broke, because they're good at starting things but not so good at finishing things.

They may have a hundred books or songs that they have started on their laptop and never finished. They may have started a few companies but have never seen a profit, because they didn't have or execute a complete plan. I know this to be true. I talk to people in these predicaments all the time. They're creators, so they're always *creating*.

We need the creators, because they are the innovators, and the innovator is always ahead of the game. My innovator examples are Steve Jobs, Walt Disney, and Richard Branson. Steve Jobs created Apple computers. Walt Disney wanted to draw; he didn't start off trying to open a theme park. Richard Branson owns two hundred companies and doesn't run any of them. These men are innovators.

> EVERYTHING STARTS WITH THE IDEA FROM THE VISIONARY—THE CREATOR, THE INNOVATOR.

If you're the innovator who has an idea you have been trying to get off the ground, but find yourself in the same place this year as last year, you need to find the rest of your team to help you move your vision forward.

THE MECHANIC

The *mechanic's* success is centered on creating systems. Mechanics are strong finishers. The mechanic can seem inflexible—like CEOs, lawyers, and accountants. My examples of mechanics are Michael Dell, Jeff Bezos, and Ray Kroc.

Michael Dell didn't create the computer, it was already created. What he did build was a system. Wealth will never manifest itself without a duplicable system. If you don't have a system, you will remain in the vicious cycle of working a job just for a paycheck.

Jeff Bezos is the founder of Amazon.com. Did he create all the products that are on that site? No, he developed an online shopping system where you can get practically anything.

Ray Kroc was not the innovator of McDonald's. He used the innovation of two brothers named Dick and Mac McDonald and built a *system* from it. Then he purchased the rights to use their name.

> THE MECHANIC IS DISTRIBUTION MINDED.
> HE CAN SHOW YOU HOW TO GET YOUR PRODUCT
> IN DIFFERENT COUNTRIES.

THE STAR

The *star* establishes a unique personal brand. Stars have magnetic personalities. They're well suited for PR (Public Relations), and they love being the center of attention. They're more concerned about image than details. They can make money very fast and spend it just as fast.

> WE NEED THE STAR BECAUSE THE STAR
> IS THE ONE WHO GETS ON THE NEWS.

Stars love the media. My examples of stars are Oprah Winfrey and Michael Jordan. Oprah became a billionaire by using a camera and a couch to talk about her weight issues. It wasn't complex at all. She got over her insecurities, followed her heart, and look what happened. Michael Jordan used his star-status, put his brand on unique tennis shoes, and made billions.

Are billions in your future, or is that too much for you to believe for?

THE SUPPORTER

The *supporter's* wealth strategy is based on building and leading high-performance teams. They spend decades behind the scenes, they're loyal to the creator, and they're great networkers. Their greatest asset is their reputation and their network. They are the glue that keeps the organization together.

My examples of supporters are Steve Ballmer and Jack Welch. The reason you may not recognize the name Steve Ballmer is because he was the number-two guy behind Bill Gates at Microsoft. He became so wealthy he bought an NBA basketball team.

Jack Welch was the president and chairman of General Electric. He did not create electricity; he was just a supporter of what already existed. You never see the supporters. They never want any glory, because they're not the stars. They probably don't care if their name is never mentioned. You truly need supporters on your team.

THE DEAL MAKER

The *deal maker's* wealth strategy is to connect people and details. They're powerful communicators and great at building relationships. The reason you need deal makers on your team is because they can make millions in a moment. They love winning and dealing. They love the *art of the deal.* The deal maker only cares about the money. Somebody needs to be on your team who's concerned solely about the money.

My example of a deal maker is Rupert Murdoch. Rupert Murdoch started Fox News, a media empire. He is known for great deals. The deal makers are always in the marketplace, and they know what to invest in. You know what that means? It guarantees that everybody stays paid up to date.

THE LANDLORD

The *landlord's* wealth strategy is controlling cash and assets. They thrive in tough economic times. While everybody else is losing houses, the landlord is gaining houses.

A Walmart near me previously occupied an 88,000 square foot facility in Georgia. It became available, and I wanted to move my operations there.

I called around to inquire about purchasing the building and found out that I couldn't buy it because Walmart didn't own it. A gentleman told me his great-grandfather bought the land in 1910 and gave it to his grandfather. Walmart knocked on his door ten years ago asking to build a store on his land. He didn't sell them the land; he leased them the land for $325,000 per month for 25 years.

So, even though Walmart moved out of the building, they still owe him $325,000 a month for the next 15 years. When I asked him what was he doing with all that money, he told me he builds hospitals, synagogues, and has sent over 17,000 kids to Ivy League schools.

God told the Israelites to possess the land; and He didn't tell them to sell it. Land is so valuable because God is not making any more! That's why we are supposed to own the land.

STAY ON THE TEAM

Each of these wealth-personalities I mentioned above brings a different dish to the table. And all the dishes make a complete meal so everyone on the team can eat. Each of them will solve a different problem for you.

> *From whom the whole body, joined and knit together by what every joint supplies, according to the effective working by which every part does its share, causes growth of the body for the edifying of itself in love.* (Ephesians 4:16 NKJV)

When every part does its share, it causes growth of the body or team. People get stuck because they are single-handedly trying to bring their vision to life while not being supported by the properly assembled team.

> YOU CANNOT SUCCEED AT HIGHER LEVELS
> AS A SOLE INDIVIDUAL.

Another thing to avoid allowing to happen along the way is the interjection of the *jealousy spirit*. If the innovator is jealous of the supporter, then discord, envy, and strife enters into the process and impedes progress. Nip the jealousy spirit in the bud, or your team and your dream will never get off the ground.

The acronym TEAM stands for *Together Everyone Accomplishes More!*

> WE ARE BETTER WHEN WE COME TOGETHER.
> TEAMWORK MAKES THE DREAM WORK.

When we work together as one, we become a *force* that can meet needs in the marketplace. Stay together. Yes, you can still be wonderful all by yourself, but you won't be effective.

MEASURE THE PERFORMANCE OF THE TEAM

Measuring is the process of collecting, analyzing, and reporting information regarding the performance of the group. It can involve studying strategies within your team to see whether the outputs are in line with what was intended or should have been achieved.

When I facilitated our largest Kings and Priests conference, there were approximately 8,000 in attendance. At a glance, you would probably measure that performance as being an A+. Well, after it was all said and done, hands were shaken, and pictures were taken, I was $95,000 in debt. So all I really had was an expensive party!

That's why you can't make assumptions on appearances, and all that glitters is not gold. Even though the event itself was a blessing to the men, the actual performance grade from the team was a D+ (debt plus headache).

In order to measure performance, you must track the progress of the strategy that was put in place. There are indicators of good performance measures that cover these four areas:

1. Financial
2. Customer
3. Process
4. People

These measures let you know whether you're on track to achieve your strategy and accomplish your objectives. Here are the KPI's (*Key Performance Indicators*) and examples.

FINANCIAL

1. **Profit.** This should be obvious, but it is still important to make note of, as this is one of the most important performance indicators on the list.
2. **Cost.** Measure cost effectiveness, and find the best ways to reduce and manage your costs.
3. **Revenue vs. Target.** This is a comparison between your actual revenue and your projected revenue. Charting and analyzing the discrepancies between these two numbers will help you identify how your business is performing.
4. **Cost of Goods Sold.** Jesus spoke to His disciples about the wisdom of counting the costs.[22] This information is key in determining how to maintain a profit and outsell your competition.

---

22 "For which of you, intending to build a tower, does not sit down first and count the cost, whether he has enough to finish it" (Luke 14:28 NKJV).

5. **Expenses vs. Budget.** Compare your actual overhead with your forecasted budget. Understanding where you actually are compared to what you budgeted helps you be more effective in future budget meetings.

CUSTOMER

1. **Customer Lifetime Value (CLV).** CLV helps you to look at the value your business is getting from a long-term customer relationship. Repeat customers give you more buck for your bang.

2. **Customer Acquisition Cost (CAC).** Divide your total acquisition costs by the number of new customers in a specific time frame. This is considered very important in e-commerce because it can help you evaluate the cost effectiveness of your marketing campaigns.

3. **Customer Satisfaction and Retention (CSR).** Make the customer happy, and they will continue to be your customer. This sounds very simple, but companies will attest to the fact that it is easier said than done. You can use multiple performance indicators to measure CSR, including customer satisfaction scores, percentage of customers repeating a purchase, and customer surveys.

4. **Net Promoter Score (NPS).** One way to determine your NPS score is to send out quarterly surveys to your customers to see how likely it is that they'll recommend your organization to someone they know.

5. **Number of Customers.** This performance indicator is fairly straightforward, as in the profit sector. When you determine the number of customers you've acquired and lost, you can better understand whether or not you are meeting your customers' needs.

> THE CUSTOMER IS NOT ALWAYS RIGHT,
> BUT SATISFYING THE CUSTOMER IS.

PROCESS

1. **Customer Support Tickets.** This is the analysis of the number of new and resolved tickets. The resolution time will help you create the best customer service experience that is worthy of good ratings.

2. **Efficiency Measure.** Efficiency is measured differently in every industry. The manufacturing of a product is a different process than providing a service that requires a different measurement tool. You can measure your manufacturing efficiency by analyzing how many units you have produced every hour, and what percentage of time your plant was up and running.

PEOPLE

1. **Employee Turnover Rate (ETR).** Do people like working for you? Does everybody quit after a few weeks or months? Having a high ETR is a deeper issue than what the surface is telling. This requires an examination of culture, environment, and personalities.

2. **Employee Satisfaction.** If you want employees and colleagues to work harder, just keep them happy. Measure your employee satisfaction through surveys and other feedback avenues to ensure good morale.

> COMING TOGETHER IS A BEGINNING.
> KEEPING TOGETHER IS PROGRESS. WORKING TOGETHER
> IS SUCCESS. —HENRY FORD

CHAPTER INSPIRATION
CHOOSE THE RIGHT PEOPLE

THE INNOVATOR
Everything starts with the idea from the visionary, the creator—the *innovator*.

- Who is the Innovator on your team?

THE MECHANIC
The *mechanic* creates systems.

- Who is the Mechanic on your team?

THE STAR
The *star* is the PR Person, the presenter, and the center of attention.

- Who is the Star on your team?

THE SUPPORTER
The *supporter* is the behind-the-scenes glue that keeps the organization together.

- Who is the Supporter on your team?

THE DEAL MAKER
The *deal maker* is the money-person who can make millions in a moment.

- Who is the Deal Maker on your team?

THE LANDLORD

The *landlord* controls the cash and assets.

- Who is the Landlord on your team?

STAY ON THE TEAM

When every part does its share, it causes growth of the body or team.

- Are you single-handedly trying to bring your vision to life while unsupported?
- Has envy or strife impeded your team's progress?
- When we work together as one, we become a force that can meet needs in the marketplace.

MEASURE THE PERFORMANCE OF THE TEAM

- Has the team delivered?
- Have you all met or exceeded expectations?
- Are you tracking the progress to know whether you're on target to achieve your strategy and accomplish your objectives?

NOTES TO REMEMBER:

CHAPTER 6

PASS THE TESTS

How badly do you want to become the person you were meant to be? Do you have what it takes to pass the required tests?

On your journey to becoming the person you were meant to be, there are certain tests that will undeniably show up in your life in some form or fashion. You must pass these tests to qualify for promotion to your next level.

The school of life can be compared to the progression we experience through the levels of education. An elementary student has to meet specific requirements to advance to high school. Successfully passing the required tests in high school prepares us for the next level—and our next test—our college entrance exam.

Being prepared is advantageous to the test-taker to maximize the opportunity presented by the test. Most people consider taking a test as a negative thing, but if you're prepared, it's a positive experience. There is a reward on the other side once you pass each test. You are taking the tests for a reason. Their purpose is to see if you are ready to handle the next level.

> BEING PREPARED MAXIMIZES THE
> OPPORTUNITY PRESENTED BY THE TEST.

TESTS OF THE CHOSEN

You're constantly being tested. In fact, you are on a training ground right now. If you are constantly failing the same tests, you'll remain stagnant and get discouraged. To stop this cycle of failing the same tests over and over, you need to become more aware of the requirements and the purpose of the tests. Then you need to make up your mind to pass whatever test comes along on your journey to becoming the person you are meant to be.

Passing the following six tests is vital to discovering what you were chosen to do and enabling you to walk in the fullness of the extraordinary person you are to become.

PATIENCE TEST

When you mention the word patience, most people automatically think it's in reference to waiting for something. However, this test comes when trials or tribulations try to rob you of your patience. If your response is to remain consistent and constant through whatever situations arise, you are passing the test. If you get anxious, nervous, frazzled, worried, or panic every time something happens, you will find yourself having to take a retest over and over again.

But let patience have its perfect work, that you may be perfect and complete, lacking nothing. (James 1:4 NKJV)

The result of patience is maturity. That word in Greek means to finish, to be complete. Finishing strong results from being patient. Patience is working on your behalf and for your good. The undesirable events that happen in your life are meant to cause you to lose patience, disrupt your consistency, and distract you from continuing to let your dreams manifest God's way.

If you lose patience you'll start doing things within your own natural ability because worry and fear have visited you and convinced you to do something about the trying event right now. Those emotions that provoked you to react are the opposite of patience. Your response should be to remain consistent when you get the unexpected phone call or negative doctor's report.

If you don't allow patience to work for you in the process of trying to get a new car, then you lie on the application and end up in a worse financial situation than you were beforehand. Now you're in debt. Had you let patience have its perfect work, as the scripture says, you may have been able to buy the car with a cash transaction.

> PASSING THE PATIENCE TEST ALLOWS
> PERFECT TIMING SO YOU CAN
> WITNESS MIRACLES AND BECOME COMPLETE,
> WHOLE, AND LACKING NOTHING.

Most people never get to the "lacking nothing" promotion this test brings because they don't let patience do its perfect work. They—especially women—think time is getting the best of them, so they put patience on the back burner. They start putting an age limit on when they want to see the manifestation of children or a husband, so then they take matters into their own hands.

And after taking things into her own hands, instead of experiencing a *happily ever after*, she's a struggling single mother or in a miserable marriage because she found a mate on *deadbeat. com.* That doesn't mean she can't recover; it means that she now has to take the scenic route on her way to becoming all she was meant to be.

Can you imagine not lacking a thing in life?

In order to achieve that status, you have to let patience do its perfect work. You are being perfected for something that you were chosen to do. When fear, anxiety, or worry knock on your door, simply let them know that visiting hours are over because you are in the middle of taking a *patience* test, and you are determined to pass it.

> THE RESULT OF PATIENCE IS PERFECTION.

HEART TEST

What is in your heart? Is something there that shouldn't be there?

When you are chosen for an assignment, it has to be a priority in your heart. There are two stories in the Bible that exemplify two really important heart tests. The first is about Abraham.

It was a really big promotion when God called Abraham to become the *father of many nations.*[23] God made certain promises to Abraham and told him that He would make his name great. Abraham was preparing for promotion, and then came the ultimate test. God told him to sacrifice his son Isaac, and the Lord gave him very specific instructions. He was to walk up the mountain, put his son on the altar and kill him. Wow! What a test!

---

23 "As for Me, behold, My covenant is with you, and you shall be a father of many nations" (Genesis 17:4 NKJV).

WHEN ABRAHAM PASSED THE HEART TEST,
GOD SPARED HIS SON.

As a chosen vessel, the *heart test* is always going to require some sacrifice on your part. It may be your money, time, or something that you love. But promotion comes when you are willing to make the sacrifice. Abraham cherished his son, but he was obedient to the instructions he was given. When Abraham passed the heart test, God not only spared his son, He fulfilled His promise through him and his descendants.

Are you holding on to something so desperately that it has taken priority over your assignment?

Your heart is the birthplace of your increase. Every successful person has had a heart test. If Abraham had not passed the heart test, he would never have experienced increase to become the father of many nations. He would have stayed in the *potential* category.

The heart test has two essential components: *trusting God*, and *obeying God*. Bill Wilson, founder of Metro World Child,[24] has a great message that focuses on Abraham and Isaac, and asks the question, "If the next thing that God asks you to do is the exact opposite of the last thing He told you, would you still trust and obey Him . . . and do it?"

Remember the narrative? Abraham and his wife Sarah were old when God told Abraham his wife was going to have a baby in their old age, and that child would be the father of a great nation. Then when the baby was older, God told Abraham to kill the boy and offer him up to God as a burnt offering.[25]

Wow! Could you have trusted and obeyed God—kill the dream, murder the legacy? Then, just as Abraham raised the knife to sacrifice his only son, God called from heaven and told

24 https://www.metroworldchild.org/
25 Genesis 22:2.

Abraham to stop and not kill his son. Each next commandment from God seemed to contradict the last.

What a heart test!

Have you ever been told you have potential? Well, it's time to graduate from having potential to being promoted to the next level. What do you do when things get rough? Abraham passed the test, and now it's your turn.

> *Above all else, guard your heart, for everything you do flows from it.* (Proverbs 4:23 NIV)

The second story is about King Solomon. He was the wealthiest and wisest man who ever lived. With all his wisdom, I believe he became intoxicated from his own success. God instructed the Israelites not to marry foreign women because they would turn their hearts away from the Lord. Solomon was disobedient, and that's exactly what happened to him.

> *For it was so, when Solomon was old, that his wives turned his heart after other gods; and his heart was not loyal to the Lord his God, as was the heart of his father David.* (1 Kings 11:4 NKJV)

> *So the Lord became angry with Solomon, because his heart had turned from the Lord God of Israel, who had appeared to him twice, and had commanded him concerning this thing, that he should not go after other gods;* [26] *but he did not keep what the Lord had commanded. Therefore, the Lord said to Solomon, "Because you have done this, and have not kept My covenant and My statutes, which I have commanded you, I will surely tear the kingdom away from you and give it to your servant."* (1 Kings 11:9-11 NKJV)

---

26 The second time God spoke to Solomon—after the dedication of the Temple—is recorded in 2 Chronicles 7:12-22. Among other things God said, He warned Solomon that he must keep God's statutes and commandments and not serve other gods (v.19).

Solomon's heart wasn't committed to God. He failed the heart test and experienced a major decrease in his life. One failed instruction can have lifetime of consequences. Every successful person gets in tough predicaments and has to make hard, character-revealing decisions.

Just as your heart is the birthplace of increase, your heart is also the birthplace of decrease. You must be intentional about guarding your heart and being obedient to the instructions of God. Then you will be on your way to experiencing increase instead of decrease in every area of your life. This is a major test to pass on the way to becoming who you were meant to be.

THE FAITH TEST

And without faith it is impossible to please God, because anyone who comes to him must believe that he exists and that he rewards those who earnestly seek him.

(Hebrews 11:6 NIV [emphasis mine])

Losing faith is one of the most unfortunate events that could happen to you. Faith pleases God, and that is clear in your *life manual*. Without faith, you lose hope and then become hopeless. When adversity presents itself, it's really a test of faith. Your *faith test* is to find out if you really believe in what you're doing.

When you stand in front of an investor, they're not really concerned about your presentation as much as you think. They want to look you in the eye to discern your own belief in yourself.

- Will you still have faith when it doesn't look like your dream is going to manifest itself?
- Are you prepared for the long haul?
- Will you have faith to hang in when things do not happen immediately?

- When your faith is tested, will you react out of desperation?
- Will you get weary or tired before you complete the journey?

EXAMPLES OF TESTS OF FAITH IN MY OWN LIFE

- When there was a negative balance in my bank account, would I still believe I was going to see increase in my life?
- When I had a meeting and the attendance was not as large as I expected, could I still believe I would be an influential speaker?
- When things weren't going according to plan, did I still believe I was chosen for a great assignment?
- Did I believe I was healed even when I did not feel well?
- Through each of these tests of faith, I held on to the promises of God, and He didn't disappoint me.

THE LOVE TEST

Let me give you a new command: Love one another. In the same way I loved you, you love one another. This is how everyone will recognize that you are my disciples—when they see the love you have for each other. (John 13:35 MSG)

The *love test* challenges you to treat people according to God's instructions. Passing the test of love requires you to be able to maintain military silence when you know you have a valid reason to verbally assault your offender. What if God hadn't given you a second chance or turned His back on you when you messed up and fell short of expectations? We are required to extend to others the same grace He gave us.[27]

---

27 "Bear with each other and forgive one another if any of you has a grievance against someone. Forgive as the Lord forgave you" (Colossians 3:13 NIV).

Expressing love in the marketplace is simply an act of serving others. No one wants to go to a business or ministry and receive bad service. The likelihood of being a repeat customer is little-to-none once we experience bad service. I love going to a restaurant that excels in the treatment of its patrons. I will even drive an extra hour and pass by many other options.

People don't just stumble into knowing how to love; they've been tested about love. When your nasty co-worker walks past you and sneers, and you still wave, smile, and say good morning, you are passing the love test. When you serve an unappreciative person and don't receive a thank you, yet you still serve them the next time with excellence, you are passing the love test. No matter who you are, you are chosen to love others.

The Word says we should owe no man anything but love.

Owe no one anything except to love one another, for he who loves another has fulfilled the law. (Romans 13:8 NKJV)

God demonstrated His own passing of the ultimate love test. He sent His only begotten Son so that we may have life and have it abundantly.[28]

THE PHYSICAL TEST

Are you preparing your physical body for the assignment at hand?

You cannot effectively fulfill what you are called to do with an unhealthy vessel. A football player can't play in the game if he is injured, he gets taken out of the game. Many leaders are letting unchecked health issues take them out of the game as well.

You need energy and strength to accomplish whatever you are chosen and called to do. I travel many days throughout the year for speaking and training engagements, and I've got to be in shape to do it. Most people don't know that one hour of teaching

28 John 3:16.

equals eight hours of physical work. I have to train my body to accomplish what I have been chosen to do. I don't want health issues to stand in my way, so I must do my part. That means I need to eat right and exercise regularly. Those are stress-reducing and body-building activities.

How many leaders have we heard about who have died before their time for health reasons?

We have the power to be healthy, so make a decision to maximize your effectiveness by training your physical body to meet the demands of what you are chosen to do. God wants us healthy so we can prosper in all we do.

> Beloved, I pray that you may prosper in all things and be in health, just as your soul prospers. (3 John 2 NKJV)

Sometimes to make a shift in our mindset, we have to process information in a different manner. We must seek to see things from God's perspective.

> Do you not know that your bodies are temples of the Holy Spirit, who is in you, whom you have received from God? You are not your own; you were bought at a price. Therefore honor God with your bodies. (1 Corinthians 6:19-20 NIV)

Do you understand what this scripture is saying? Your body is a temple that houses the Holy Spirit, and you are to honor God with your body. In other words, when you don't take proper care of yourself, you are not honoring God. Ouch! I hope this revelation empowers you to make adjustments in the area of health and wellness. It is beneficial to you and those who love you.

THE MONEY TEST

We all need money to fulfill our assignment. Most people don't have an *income* problem, they have a *money management* problem.

We need to become expert managers of the money we have, and then we can experience increase.

Money is a seed. You must be faithful with the seed. You can either eat the seed or plant it. You can invest it for the future or you can spend it on your present. Most people don't have seed, or cash flow, because they spend it on their *present*. The money test comes to deliver you from material things. People fail the money test because of financial lust. They have acquired a lot of debt from trying to accumulate things they haven't yet earned.

> IF YOU PLANT A SEED, YOU
> CAN CONTROL THE ENTIRE FOREST.

Can God trust you with one million dollars?

I had to answer that question ten years ago, and the answer was no. If I would have obtained one million dollars on a Monday, I would have bought a new house for at least two other people, purchased thirty pairs of new shoes, five new cars, and would have been broke and depleted by Friday.

God couldn't trust me yet with the life He designed for me because I was stuck in financial lust. I wasn't a good steward over my finances. My spending habits exceeded my income.

I contributed to my church and gave to charity every now and then. I only obeyed God with my money sometimes. God is not a fair-weather God. And you're either with Him or you're not. You're in or out. You're going to be obedient or disobedient. Either He can trust you or He can't.

We don't ask God what He wants us to do with our paycheck because we really don't want to hear what He has to say.

Your blessing is on the other side of your obedience. Managed as God desires, your money leaves your hand, but it doesn't leave your life. It enters your future. Your obedience will bless generations to come. Giving is not about your money, it's about your heart. God wants to ensure your heart is with Him so He can get more to you. That's a hard lesson that I had to learn.

God was trying to get something to me, but I had the wrong heart.

You ask and do not receive, because you ask amiss, that you may
spend it on your pleasures. (James 4:3 NKJV)

What are your motives when you ask for a new car? Is it to be able to pick someone up to give them a ride? Is it for your pleasure solely to ride around in and look prosperous?

If you need transportation there is nothing wrong with asking for it, but examine your motives for that car and every luxury you desire.

About twenty-five years ago all I wanted was a new BMW. Financial lust was the culprit, and the evidence of that was the fact that I fell three months behind on my payments. I confided in a friend and told my friend there was no way I could let my car go. This friend advised me to put my car in their garage the first day, then take it to the McDonald's parking lot the second day, and on the third day park it at the church parking lot.

There was no way the "Repo Man" would get my car from church.

Well, ladies and gentlemen, just as Jesus arose on the third day, so did my car. I was so embarrassed, but after the initial shock, there was so much peace that followed. I was focused on a new BMW when God had a whole new life waiting for me, in which I would be able to buy the entire car lot, not just one car. God wants us to have financial abundance.

The *money test* is where a lot of people get in trouble and miss the mark because they haven't properly categorized the use of it. Money is a tool to use in carrying out your calling. It's used to help others, to meet your needs, and to invest. Money is an amplifier of whatever is in your heart. If your heart is evil, you will use money for bad things. If your heart is right, you will use money for good things. Money is also for you to enjoy.

Money is a *test* of your faithfulness and character. It is a *testimony* of your giving. There are over 2,350 Scriptures in the Bible on how to handle money and possessions.

Passing the money test involves bringing your spending in line with your income. You need a family spending plan inclusive of deleting impulsive spending, examining motives for making a purchase, seeking wise counsel, surrounding yourself with people who are smarter than you financially, and asking them for advice.

10 COMMANDMENTS OF WEALTHY LIVING

Create a wealthy environment and mindset at home. Print out the following ten commandments of wealthy living and have your family sign it.

1. I will live within my means.
2. I will maximize my income potential through educational training.
3. I will effectively manage my credit, debt, and tax obligations.
4. I will save at least 10 percent of my earnings.
5. I will use home ownership as a foundation of building wealth.
6. I will devise an investment plan for my retirement and my children's college education.
7. I will ensure my entire family adheres to a sensible spending plan.
8. I will support the creation of small businesses.
9. I will guarantee my wealth is passed on to the next generation through adequate insurance and estate planning.
10. I will strengthen my local church through consistent giving.

Build wealth in increments using the 10/10/10 plan: Give 10 percent to savings. Give 10 percent to God, And invest 10 percent in yourself. I suggest you get my bestselling book, *Never Chase A Paycheck Again*. It will help you tremendously with your finances and wealth.

Contrary to popular belief, money is not wealth. Wealth is anything that can be handed down from generation to generation. Wealth is an attitude, a mindset, and a business idea. It's not tangible, you can't see wealth.

> *So if you have not been trustworthy in handling worldly wealth, who will trust you with true riches?* (Luke 16:11 NIV)

If you have not been faithful with money, how can you be trusted with true riches? True riches are not houses, cars, red-bottomed shoes, or fine jewelry. It's the favor, peace, wisdom, and knowledge of God. You must pass the money test to get those true riches.

CHAPTER INSPIRATION
PASS THE TESTS

How badly do you want to become the person you were meant to be? Do you have what it takes to pass the required tests?

PATIENCE TEST
The result of patience is perfection.

- Are you willing to patiently wait to receive God's best for you?

But let patience have its perfect work, that you may be perfect and complete, lacking nothing   (James 1:4 NKJV)

HEART TEST

Abraham passed the test.

- Is your heart dedicated to God's plan for your life or your own plan?

Above all else, guard your heart, for everything you do flows from it.   (Proverbs 4:23 NIV)

FAITH TEST

We are not supposed to get desperate or anxious when trials come.

- Is your faith still intact when tested in your health, finances, family, and ministry?

But without faith it is impossible to please Him, for he who comes to God must believe that He is, and that He is a rewarder of those who diligently seek Him.   (Hebrews 11:6 NKJV)

LOVE TEST

Treat others as God has commanded. Serve with love and compassion.

- Are you able to love people who don't deserve your love?
- Can you do business with someone who isn't like you?
- Can you serve them with love?
- What about the person who talks negatively about you?

Owe no one anything except to love one another, for he who loves another has fulfilled the law. (Romans 13:8 NKJV)

PHYSICAL TEST

You cannot be as effective as you should be with an unhealthy vessel.

- Are you preparing your physical body for the assignment at hand?
- Make a decision to honor God by taking good care of your body.

Do you not know that your bodies are temples of the Holy Spirit, who is in you, whom you have received from God? You are not your own; you were bought at a price. Therefore honor God with your bodies. (1 Corinthians 6:19-20 NIV)

Beloved, I pray that you may prosper in all things and be in health, just as your soul prospers. (3 John 2 NKJV)

MONEY TEST

Most people don't have an income problem, they have a management problem. Passing the money test involves bringing your spending in line with your income.

- Does your family have a spending plan that:
  - Deletes impulsive spending?
  - Includes examining motives for making a purchase?
  - Makes use of wise counsel?
  - Involves surrounding yourself with people who are smarter than you financially and asking them for advice?

- Did you print out the ten commandments of wealthy living and have your family sign it?
- Have you been trustworthy with your money?

So if you have not been trustworthy in handling worldly wealth, who will trust you with true riches? (Luke 16:11 NIV)

NOTES TO REMEMBER:

CHAPTER 7

BECOME THE PERSON YOU WERE MEANT TO BE

The world is waiting on you.

For the earnest expectation of the creature waiteth for the manifestation of the sons of God. (Romans 8:19 KJV)

USE YOUR GIFT FOR GOOD

Let's use the comic book characters Batman and Joker for an illustration. One is using his gift for good. The other one is using his gift for evil. Both of them could be a hero to a certain network of people. Both are talented, and both are skilled communicators. They both know how to wield their influence against each other.

Some people have those same conflicts. For example, why did the pastor become corrupt? How does a lifetime bank robber transform his life and become good? These are great conundrums of how people may start out good and end up bad, and how some bad people change their lives for the good.

When you are settled about becoming the person you were meant to be, you've first got to recognize that you do have a gift, that you do have value, and that you do have something to offer the world. You can use that gift for good, or you can use it for evil. In order to become the person you were meant to be, you have to be intentional about using your gift for good. It's better to give than receive.

As I traveled through life on my journey to becoming the man I am today, I was in a place of frustration. I didn't know who I was or what I was supposed to be doing in life or business. I had to get alone in a place of prayer and seclusion. I had to fast, read, and study the Word of God. I cut out all the other noise, and I was alone with my thoughts.

I had to dig deep within myself, uncover everything obvious and hidden, and examine who I really was—the good, the bad, and the ugly. There were areas that I was ashamed of, and there were good things that I liked about myself. What I realized was that my gift was consistent and constant.

Your gift is divine; it's the blessing of God that's in you. It's perfectly tailored and custom-made according to your personality and the way God crafted you. You can't work for your gift; you just discover it and receive it. You can use it to satisfy your flesh or use it to serve others.

Your gift is perfect because it comes from God. That doesn't mean your character couldn't use a little fine-tuning. Don't be the pastor who attracts large crowds but who, behind closed doors, is meaner than a leashed dog—or who preaches one thing but does another.

Sexual misconduct cases have sprung up from years prior against powerful men who were gifted but whose characters and morals were questionable. They were misusing the power that came from their gifts, and it overshadowed any good that was done. If you lead with your gift and leave your character behind, you will be exposed. Examine yourself and make the necessary adjustments. Use your gift for good, and you will receive the corresponding harvest for the good seeds you are sowing.

EMPOWER OTHERS

Everyone has an empowering gift—no matter the size of the audience your gift is for. If you have a lawn care business, you should want to use your gift to be the best lawn care maintenance professional on the planet. Just looking at my grass used to give me a headache, but the guy who cut my grass took delight in the task.

In becoming the person you were meant to be, your vision should include solving a problem or helping someone. In doing so, you are empowering others. You do not want to be known for the problems you create. When you are known for the problems you solve, you will be in demand.

Professionally speaking, being known as a problem solver will affect the income you'll receive. Spiritually speaking, as long as you perform your duties with excellence, no matter how big or small they may be, you will be empowering the onlookers or recipients with your gift.

Every smile and interaction can change the course of someone else's day. You can be influential in a positive or negative way. Empowering others is an important act of kindness you can do for your fellow man.

Empowering Ways:

- Complimenting and not criticizing.
- Not being judgmental.
- Praising any progress—big or small.
- Suppressing your ego.
- Giving others the feeling they are loved.
- Treating people like you want to be treated. All occupations, whether it's the janitor, cashier, car wash attendant, or others, are occupied by people like you, so treat them accordingly
- Smiling and thanking people for their services.

I've learned that people will forget what you said, people will forget what you did, but people will never forget how you made them feel.   —Maya Angelou

EMPOWERING OTHERS ALSO EMPOWERS US.
IT'S A WIN-WIN FOR ALL WHO ARE INVOLVED.

GO FROM POTENTIAL TO GROWTH TO MANIFESTATION

I believe the most frustrated man or woman reading this book is the one who is living on the island called *Potential*. While the island may be aesthetically pleasing, it is dangerous and unproductive to live there. Everyone is born with potential, and the good thing is that it gives us a constant reminder of what is possible.

However, there's a big difference between potential and manifestation. Most people stay in the realm of what they could potentially do, which is a very frustrating place to be. Potential by itself can't pay any bills or leave an inheritance for the next generation.

Your focus should be on how to grow from potential to manifestation. Surround yourself with things that promote your growth, like books and recordings from motivational speakers. You have to read, study, and then do something with what you discover. Faith without action will keep you stuck in what you could potentially have or be.

You have to grow up, to go up.

One of the reasons many people don't fulfill their potential is that they are involved in activities that point them in the opposite direction of what they are called to be. For example, you may have the potential of being a great writer, but you are remaining in an unrewarding occupation as a waitress. That job may be rewarding to someone else, but it will never be to you, because your energy is being diverted into accommodating hungry customers instead of creating interesting characters.

However, if you are the parking lot attendant with the potential to be a great musical artist, and while you are watching cars you are practicing vocal arrangements, you're using your time wisely. We all have the same amount of time in a day, so use your hours and minutes to grow in the direction you want to go.

Michael Jordan had the potential to be one of the greatest basketball players ever when he was in high school. It wasn't until he experienced growth through a relentless practice schedule and played in the NBA that he achieved that status. He was in the gym when other players were still in the bed. He was intentional on *growing* into one of the greatest basketball players to ever play the game. I am sure he had to disappoint some people and make adjustments to his schedule to accommodate his growth, but he remained focused on the goal.

Do you think the caterpillar *became* a butterfly? No, the caterpillar was already a butterfly from birth. We couldn't witness the physical manifestation of a graceful beautiful butterfly until it transformed from a stubby crawling caterpillar. That growth process didn't happen overnight, and the same goes for you.

The transformation of a caterpillar into a butterfly is absolutely fascinating and is similar to your process. You must go through phases of shedding skin, which is synonymous to getting rid of old ideas and habits. The reality is that the caterpillar was a baby butterfly the whole time!

You are a baby entrepreneur changing into a territorial leader, franchise owner, real estate mogul, or whatever it is God has chosen you to grow into. Just as the beautiful butterfly has to go through an amazing life cycle, you too must evolve into the amazing person you were created to be in order to pass along your legacy.

The metamorphosis process may even surprise you. As the great T.D. Jakes always says, "Get ready; get ready; get ready!"

AGE IS INEVITABLE, BUT GROWTH IS NOT.

Getting ready means you have to position yourself for growth. Here are six things you can do to get ready:

1. **Practice saying "No."** "No" is a complete sentence that will keep you from wasting time and energy that will not result in growth.
2. **Clarify your plan on paper.** I cannot emphasize enough that you need a plan for how to grow from point A to Z.
3. **Talk less.** The people who do the most talking have the least action. Practice active listening.
4. **Become an expert in one thing.** FOCUS is an acronym for *Follow One Course Until Successful.*
5. **Forgive yourself.** Everyone has regrets. Move past your disappointment, forgive yourself, release it, and move forward.

6. **Set one major financial goal.** Setting a major financial goal will help you to grow. Once you achieve it, you will no longer be in the *potential* category. You will have moved to manifestation.

> FOCUS ON GROWTH, AND
> MANIFESTATION WILL FOLLOW.

SELL YOURSELF TO THE WORLD

For those of you who just imagined that I am telling you to assume the persona of a used car salesman, you may now exhale. I was not suggesting that you have to disguise your flaws and convince a buyer to purchase *you* at a discount. The good thing about this type of selling is that it doesn't require asking anybody for a monetary exchange.

The average person will cringe at the thought of sales. The reason has nothing to do with a lack of marketing education or experience; it's the mere fact that they are afraid of rejection.

The reality is that we are all in the sales business! As you go about your day-to-day routine, you are convincing someone to buy into something that you either do or believe. You haven't categorized it as selling, but it is. If you are a parent, at some point in your child's toddler years you had to employ secret-service tactics to get the little prince or princess to open wide so you could airplane-in a forkful of vegetables.

You couldn't pat yourself on the back for that moment of success, though, because the mission was not accomplished. Through all the child's faces of disgust, you had to use special sales skills to convince that miniature human to chew and swallow. I can imagine you used an elementary version of the *healthy* sales pitch to explain the importance of fiber consumption.

When you tell your friends about the awesome movie you just viewed and suggest they spend their dollars to experience the emotional rollercoaster you just took in, your excitement provoked them to check for the times of the next showings. You just sold a movie ticket for XYZ Theaters and didn't receive a commission.

After you have feasted at an exquisite restaurant, you can't wait to tell your colleagues to try the Aged Rib Eye. When they do so and come back to tell you how much they enjoyed it, you just sold an expensive dinner for ABC Restaurant and didn't receive a commission.

WHEN YOU PERFORM YOUR JOB DUTIES,
YOUR LEVEL OF EXCELLENCE IS YOUR SALES TOOL
FOR PROMOTION TO THE NEXT LEVEL.

You are selling something every day. Imagine if you took that same enthusiasm for someone else's product, business, or service and directed that energy to sell *yourself*. You cannot use your gift for good if no one knows about it. I want you to sell yourself to the world by being a walking, talking, moving miracle display of what you were chosen to do.

Everyone who hears your name or sees your face should know what you were put on this earth to do because they see your fruit. You are God's trophy.

TO SELL YOURSELF TO THE WORLD,
YOU HAVE TO BE *PASSIONATE.*

Have you ever seen me speaking at one of my leadership meetings? Have you ever watched an NBA coach give instructions in a championship game? What about Oprah Winfrey's acceptance speech at the Golden Globes?

The common denominator with world-renowned, successful people is the driving force used to deliver their gifts to us. That is called passion. If you are not passionate about your pursuit of becoming all that you are called to be and do, you will continue to fly under the radar and miss opportune moments that were designed to catapult you toward the bullseye of your destiny.

Just like an animal on a hunt for prey, your passion should be able to be sniffed out. The people who are assigned to you are attracted to the scent of your passion, and they will find you.

Here are three other traits of a good salesman for you to use to deliver your gift to the world.

1. **Knowledge.** A knowledgeable person is respected and well received. You may be naturally gifted in one or more areas, but there is always room for growth. I am a natural at speaking and teaching. However, I have great mentors, and I consistently study how I can better myself. I am always in a posture of growing. Humble people recognize there is always something to learn, and the things you are taught can come from the least likely person.

   Study to shew thyself approved unto God, a workman that needeth not to be ashamed, rightly dividing the word of truth.
   (2 Timothy 2:15 KJV)

2. **Presentation Skills.** I am not talking about standing in front of a room of people and giving a speech. You are subliminally giving out information about yourself all day long, and you need to be aware of it. Your attire, your conversation, your social media posts and "likes," and your response to adversity are your own PowerPoint slides. To *disseminate* information means to *give out.* To *communicate* means to *get through.* The point of your presentation is to *communicate*—to get your

ideas and concepts *through* to people who come in contact with you, whether in word or deed.

3. **Closing Ability.** Unlike the used car salesman, you don't have to pressure anybody to sign on the dotted line. Your gift will make room for you. God has already closed the deal.

> *A man's gift makes room for him, and brings him before great men.* (Proverbs 18:16 NASB)

WALK IN GOD'S PERFECT WILL FOR YOUR LIFE

Are you really called to do it?

Now that you are ready to do what you believe you are chosen to do, the victory of the rest of your days has everything to do with the answer to the above question. Do not be afraid of the answer. It's best to settle this right now, so you can use the practical and spiritual advice in this book to steer you in the direction of *His perfect will—not your desired will.*

Do you know that you can be successfully wrong?

Anyone can start a business or pursue an acting career. There are too many seemingly successful individuals who are living an unfulfilled life. The evidence lies in the number of celebrity suicides and the unprecedented increase in anti-depressant prescriptions.

The blessing of God is in His perfect will for your life. Provision is guaranteed. Peace will flow like a river. And your energy will jump-start your day.

> *As for God, His way is perfect; the word of the Lord is proven; He is a shield to all who trust in Him.* (Psalm 18:30 NKJV)

The only thing that's perfect in your life is your assignment. God has a tailor-made suit for you. If you tried on someone else's it would be too tight and vice versa.

Many desire to do God's will, but they struggle because they're not sure what God's will is for them. Sometimes, we need to just stop and ask God to give us wisdom to discern His will.

> *If any of you lacks wisdom, you should ask God, who gives generously to all without finding fault, and it will be given to you.*   (James 1:5 NIV)

EXPECT THE GREATER

There is something on the inside of you that God has placed there to enable you to be a world changer. The treasure that's in you is designed to bless the nations. I am challenging you to be better so you can *expect the greater*. Jesus said we would do greater works than He did while He was here on the earth. That means He has given you exactly what you need to release and manifest the potential that is within you.

> *Most assuredly, I say to you, he who believes in Me, the works that I do he will do also; and greater works than these he will do, because I go to My Father.*   (John 14:12 NKJV)

My desire is to pull every gift and morsel of talent out of you and get it out there into this world. My good friend and mentor, the late Myles Munroe, said:

> The wealthiest places in the world are not gold mines, oil fields, diamond mines or banks. The wealthiest place is the cemetery. There lies companies that were never started, masterpieces that were never painted . . ... In the cemetery there is buried the greatest treasure of untapped potential.

There is a treasure within you that must come out. Don't go to the grave with your treasure still within YOU.[29]

That's not going to happen to you!

Will you let these practices and principles assist in ushering you into your desired destiny by putting them in action?

Be intentional because there is a God-infused opportunity in every moment that is hidden in plain view. Moments can be missed, maximized, or managed. Angels have been given charge to orchestrate the affairs of your life by giving you directions to take you to the next level. I believe this book is being used as an angelic instructional tool for you.

In life you will have failures, challenges, and mistakes, but He has already declared the end of your life from the beginning. So stay on course, and you will not fail what God has intended for you.

Declaring the end from the beginning, And from ancient times things that are not yet done, Saying, "My counsel shall stand, And I will do all My pleasure." (Isaiah 46:10 NKJV)

God has called you to something, and He doesn't want you to be passive regarding the Kingdom-business He has chosen and assigned you to do. I believe you are thirsty and hungry for your assignment to manifest. I pray that this book has lit a fire in you, and you will not abort your mission.

So he called ten of his servants, delivered to them ten minas, and said to them, "Do business till I come." (Luke 19:13 NKJV)

God has given you instructions to do business for Him while you are here on this earth. One thing you can count on is that if God tells you to do something, He has given you what you need

---

29 > > > > *THERE WAS NO FOOTNOTE SOURCE LISTED IN THE MS*

to accomplish it with excellence! You are a marketplace-minister, and your goal is to produce results. God has called you to use your gifts, talents, and skills, so you must take them off the shelf of mediocrity.

It's time to make your next move. This is your year of execution, boldness, enterprise, and power, but you are going to need to have the audacity to implement your BIG idea!

In Proverbs we read that a good person leaves an inheritance for their children's children.[30] Your big idea can produce generational blessings for years to come! It's time for you to occupy the land that was prepared for you, literally and spiritually. You are to step out and take care of business. There are to be no more excuses and no more delays. God needs you to step up, and He wants you on fire.

God has called me to do more than just sit in a pew. He told me to empower and educate people, and He promised He would give me the resources to be a *distribution center*. You are the remnant whom I have been called and chosen to assist in manifesting your life-vision.

You are anointed and backed by God. God used people in the Bible to solve a financial issue in the marketplace, and He wants to use you to do the same. You have purpose, and you are very important to the Kingdom's family business!

Most people only expect the mundane or average because they think how normal people think. You have to believe you are great. No problem in your life is bigger than the solution inside of you. Your escape out of your situation starts with expecting things to get better and expecting yourself to be greater.

God told Abraham that He was going to make his name great, and that applies to you, too. I believe you are going to leave your

---

30 "A good man leaves an inheritance to his children's children, but the wealth of the sinner is stored up for the righteous" (Proverbs 13:22 NKJV).

footprint in this world and a lasting legacy for the next generation. Every person you encounter will leave your presence improved because they experienced the essence of the gift within you.

Humility doesn't mean that you're shy or quiet. It means you are stepping into your greatness with humble confidence.

God has given you a vision, ideas, a sound mind, Kingdom assets, health, peace, the ability to think soberly, the Holy Spirit, and the gift of faith. You are chosen to put these assets in operation. After you have followed the plan set for you in this book, you can expect the greater.

The greatness in you will emerge, and your gift will not be denied any longer. Your circle of influence will take notice of the *new you.* You are chosen and are becoming who you were meant to be.

This is what I believe for you:

- Restoration of things you lost
- Peace of mind
- An unconditional love life
- The hurt of past years to fade
- Promotion and increase
- Unexpected income
- To be in great demand

This book is to challenge you to expect the greater. You're not who everybody else says you are. You are becoming who you were meant to be.

Get excited about your future! God wants you to walk in your greatness. Greatness arrives when you complete God's plan for your life and satisfy divine expectations.

You will be unstoppable. You'll experience double grace, double favor, supernatural healing, miracles, signs, and wonders as you walk into this new season of self-discovery. Others will

CHOSEN

inhale the aroma of *true wealth* when you enter a room. No good thing will God withhold from you as you walk uprightly.

You are *chosen*. You are becoming the person you were meant to be, and you will bear good fruit that shall remain!

> *You did not choose Me, but I chose you and appointed you that you should go and bear fruit, and that your fruit should remain, that whatever you ask the Father in My name He may give you.*
> (John 15:16 NKJV)

— CHAPTER INSPIRATION —
BECOME THE PERSON YOU WERE MEANT TO BE

USE YOUR GIFT FOR GOOD

When you are settled about becoming the person you were meant to be, you've first got to recognize that you do have a gift, that you do have value, and that you do have something to offer the world. You can use that gift for good, or you can use it for evil. In order to become the person you were meant to be, you have to be intentional about using your gift for good.

- What is your gift?
- How will you use that gift to do good?

EMPOWER OTHERS

Everyone has an empowering gift, no matter the size of the audience that your gift is for. In becoming the person you were meant to be, your vision should include solving a problem or helping someone. Empowering others is an important act of kindness that you can do for your neighbor or fellow man.

108

- What problem is using your gift going to solve?
- What act of kindness can you do today?

I've learned that people will forget what you said, people will forget what you did, but people will never forget how you made them feel."
— Maya Angelou

GO FROM POTENTIAL TO GROWTH TO MANIFESTATION

Everyone is born with potential. There's a difference between potential and manifestation, and most people stay in the realm of what they could *potentially* do, which is a very frustrating place to be.

- Is your focus on growth?
- Have you surrounded yourself with things that promote your growth?
- Remember, you need to grow up to go up.

SELL YOURSELF TO THE WORLD

I want you to sell yourself to the world by being a walking, talking, moving miracle display of what you were chosen to do.

- Does everyone who hears your name or sees your face know what you were put on this earth to do?

WALK IN GOD'S PERFECT WILL FOR YOUR LIFE

The blessing of God is in His perfect will for your life and should be obvious by the provision, peace, and energy you are experiencing.

- Are you experiencing provision?
- Is peace flowing like a river in your life?
- Does passion for what you are doing jump start your day?
- The simplicity and sweatless victory of the rest of your days has everything to do with whether you are in His will or your own will.

As for God, His way is perfect; the word of the Lord is proven; He is a shield to all who trust in Him. (Psalm 18:30 NKJV)

EXPECT THE GREATER

God has called you to a great work, and He doesn't want you to be passive regarding the Kingdom-business He has *chosen* and assigned you to do.

- Are you thirsty and hungry for your assignment to manifest?
- Are you ready to occupy the land that was prepared for you, literally and spiritually?
- Are you *expecting the greater?*

NOTES TO REMEMBER:

Go from Nobody to *Chosen!*

ABOUT ROBERT J. WATKINS

Robert J. Watkins is a twenty-year entrepreneur, best-selling author, and the leader of Conquer Worldwide. He is on a mission to create two million jobs by resourcing two hundred thousand new entrepreneurs in two hundred cities. For over twenty-five years, he has empowered, educated, and financed thousands of new leaders to economically and financially impact their communities.

Conquer Worldwide LLC
8491 Hospital Drive, Suite 121
Douglasville, GA 30134

Facebook: @drrobertjwatkins   Tel: 1.888.526.1118
Instagram: robertjwatkins   Fax: 1.404.601.9692
Twitter: robertjwatkins   www.ConquerWorldwide.com
LinkedIn: drrobertjwatkins

BEAUTY FROM ASHES
Donna Sparks

In a transparent and powerful manner, the author reveals how the Lord took her from the ashes of a life devastated by failed relationships and destructive behavior to bring her into a beautiful and powerful relationship with Him. The author encourages others to allow the Lord to do the same for them.

Donna Sparks is an Assemblies of God evangelist who travels widely to speak at women's conferences and retreats. She lives in Tennessee.

www.story-of-grace.com

www.facebook.com/
   donnasparksministries/

https://www.facebook.com/
   AuthorDonnaSparks/

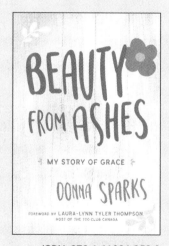

ISBN: 978-1-61036-252-8

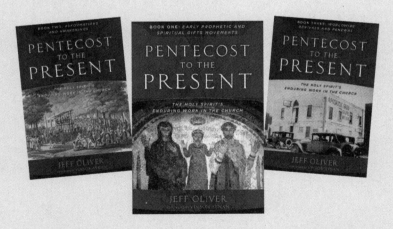